Gullah Branches, West African Roots

Gullah Branches,
West African Roots

Ronald Daise

SANDLAPPER PUBLISHING CO., INC.
ORANGEBURG, SOUTH CAROLINA USA

First Edition

Published by Sandlapper Publishing Co., Inc.
    Orangeburg, South Carolina USA

Manufactured in the United States of America

Photographs used by permission.

Texts within this book are from productions scripted and performed by Ronald Daise: "My Soul Been Bless! Gullah Roots, Branches, Blossoms," (© 2005 by Ronald Daise); "MAKE A DIFFERENCE! (Lessons from Africa to You)" (© 2005 by Ronald Daise); "Priscilla's Posse, A Press Conference about Gullah Heritage" (© 2005 by Ronald Daise); and "Gullah/ Geechee Rhythms" (© 2005 by Ronald Daise). www.gullahgullah.com

"Mother to Son," © 1994 by The Estate of Langston Hughes, from *The Collected Poems of Langston Hughes*. Used by permission of Alfred A. Knopf, a division of Random House, Inc.

All text in this volume written by Ronald Daise unless otherwise noted.

Front cover art, "Mandala I," by Natalie Daise. Used by permission of the artist. Photograph by Sue Jarrett.

Library of Congress Cataloging-in-Publication Data

Daise, Ronald.
    Gullah branches, West African roots / Ronald Daise. — 1st ed.
        p. cm.
    Includes bibliographical references.
    ISBN 978-0-87844-182-2 (pbk. : alk. paper)
  1. African Americans—South Carolina—Saint Helena Island—Social
life and customs. 2. Gullahs—South Carolina—Saint Helena Island—Social
life and customs. 3. Saint Helena Island (S.C.)—Social life and
customs. 4. Africa, West—Social life and customs. 5. Africa,
West—Description and travel. 6. Daise, Ronald—Travel—Africa, West. 7. Daise,
Ronald—Family. 8. African diaspora. 9. Gullahs—Poetry. 10. Africa,
West—Poetry. I. Title.

F277.B3D348 2007
305.896'0730973—dc22

2006102114

ACKNOWLEDGEMENTS

Immense gratitude to my bride and friend Natalie for helping me fine-tune the vision for this book; Natalie, Sara, and Simeon for allowing me to be away from home for long stretches of time to gain wonderful experiences to share with others; my mom, Kathleen G. Daise, for recalling lines and melodies of old spirituals; Congressman James E. Clyburn for sponsoring the Gullah/Geechee Cultural Heritage Corridor bill and perservering throughout its legislation, and for writing this book's Foreword; the "Teaching and Learning in Ghana 2004" coordinators and participants; Linda Krauer, Beaufort High School English Department head for posting the "TLG in Ghana 2004" flier in the workroom and encouraging me to participate; Earl and Barbara Larsen; Pastor David Holland and the Tidal Creek Fellowship members, Missions Ministries and Praise Team, Eugene and Vermelle Matthews, Linda Connor, Wayne and Alex Grabenbauer, Babette Bloch, Emory Campbell and Gullah Heritage Consulting Services, Shikira B. Williams (Sprauve), N'Kia Jones (Campbell), and Brookgreen Gardens Board of Trustees member Joan Coker for contributing toward my trip to Sierra Leone; Bob Jewell, president and CEO of Brookgreen Gardens, for affording me the opportunity to represent Brookgreen abroad; Joe Opala for inviting me for a second time to participate in a Gullah homecoming to Sierra Leone and for proofreading my manuscript; members of "Priscilla's Posse" for being exquisite stitchings upon a tapestry of memories that will last forever; the agencies and individuals who permitted me to use photographs and kindly indulged my requests to submit and then re-submit them in the appropriate formats; my sis, Irene, for encouraging me to "Think of a plan, Ron!" and supporting funding for DNA analysis to determine our family's ancestral heritage; the late Pete Covington who told me almost two decades ago that while undergoing a heart attack he'd had a vision that I would one day do something of importance to African Americans and black people everywhere; Minister Ruthie Herriott for prophesying and telling me to receive it; Amanda Gallman, publisher, and Barbara Stone, editor and production manager, for wholehearted support of and excitement about this project; and, ultimately, God for working all things together in His own time.

FOREWORD

Although my three years as a public school teacher in Charleston, South Carolina, and more than forty-five years of marriage to a native of Gullah heritage have developed in me much more than a mere fascination with the culture, when Ron Daise approached me about writing the foreword for this book, I felt a bit inadequate. I wondered if there was anything I could add to the body of knowledge developed by Ron in *Gullah Branches, West African Roots*. But I learned from reading this magnificent publication that however limited one's experiences may be with this grand slice of Americana, each of us has something to contribute to preserving and protecting the Gullah culture.

I demonstrated my commitment to this effort five years ago when I introduced legislation authorizing and funding the National Park Service to conduct a study of the Gullah culture. The results of that two-year project led me to propose legislation to create the Gullah/Geechee Cultural Heritage Corridor. That legislation establishes a commission and creates a pool of funding that will be utilized in education and preservation efforts for the endangered culture—Gullah in North and South Carolina, and Geechee in Georgia and Florida. I believe this book makes an extraordinary contribution to preserving this rich heritage for future generations.

I was particularly struck by Ron's personal transformation from being ashamed of his Gullah heritage to embracing its value and making it his life's work. This is a journey that many Gullah descendants have taken and many more continue to struggle with today. We live in a society that seems to place a higher value on sameness than it does on the diversity that makes us the envy of the world. For years we tried to assimilate other cultures to make them more "American." Such efforts have stripped our country of much of the unique tapestry that has been woven by our differences.

Gullah Branches, West African Roots is an unabashed celebration of a vibrant culture. Through the eyes of Ron Daise, we experience the daily life of Gullah people past and present. We can almost hear the sounds of Negro spirituals ringing in our ears, feel the romantic language of the Gullah people rolling off our tongues, taste the curried rice and other sea island delicacies, and see the rich colors that express such deep meaning within Gullah traditions.

Ron has exposed the beauty of a once closeted culture and compelled his audience with a sense of urgency to preserve it. This work inspires pride in those with Gullah roots, those previously shamed by others outside and even within their own families. Ron is telling their story and the story of their ancestors. It is a story of faith, of courage, and of character.

We meet Priscilla and her great-great-great-great-great-granddaughter, Thomalind Martin Polite. We are with them as their journey comes full circle from Priscilla's capture in Sierra Leone to Thomalind's triumphant return to her ancestral homeland. We follow the struggle of the Gullah people to finally realize their dream of a Gullah Bible, so they may experience reading the *New Testament* in their native tongue.

We see a day in the life of enslaved Africans on a rice plantation in coastal South Carolina and learn of the Gullah customs surrounding life and death. We see the journey of Gullah people, who come face to face in West Africa, seeing for the first time outside their family "people who look just like me." I have experienced those emotions.

The theme woven throughout is that there remain strong connections between the Gullah people and their roots in Western Africa. The language, often misrepresented as "broken English," is so similar to its African roots, Gullah can be understood by African dignitaries visiting Penn Center today. Gullah people visiting West Africa see traditions from their youth still being used in their homeland. And there is always the common bond of the Negro spiritual that binds the two together no matter the distance through time and space.

By drawing these links, Ron dispels the myth that Gullah is the culture of slavery. It is a culture rooted in West Africa, brought to America by enslaved Africans and blended with European languages and customs. It is a culture with value that was captured by white European Americans seeking to cultivate the rice plantations they owned, but needing the knowledge and skills of African natives to make them successful. This is a powerful story, one that turns what was once the embarrassment of having enslaved ancestors to one that demonstrates the value of their ancestors' talents and treasures.

This is a story of hope that breaks the literal and figurative bonds of slavery. Ron has thoughtfully and thoroughly documented the journey of the Gullah culture and instilled pride in all those of Gullah/Geechee heritage. His anecdotes are compelling and artfully weaved, much like the sweetgrass baskets that have come to symbolize the Gullah culture. I commend him on this extraordinary book, and I would recommend it as a "must read" for students in South Carolina schools.

Congressman James E. Clyburn
December 29, 2006

PREFACE

Gullah culture thrives along the coastal and immediate inland communities of South Carolina, Georgia, southern North Carolina, and northern Florida. The cultural branches of Gullahs, or Geechees (as we're also called) – physical features, dietary practices, language and/or tonality, spirituality, beliefs, crafts, and customs – are rooted in West African heritage. Like the vibrancy and verdancy of marsh grass in the tidal creeks and swamps of Gullah communities throughout the summertime, awareness and appreciation of Gullah culture in the world community has grown lush.

U.S. Congressman James E. Clyburn, D-South Carolina, in 2005, proposed a $20 million bill to protect the Gullah way of life through establishing a Gullah/Geechee Cultural Heritage Corridor. The legislation would provide for three interpretive centers – two in South Carolina and one in Georgia – to explain Gullah culture for visitors. It also would provide for building restoration and other projects.

In 2004 The National Trust for Historic Preservation named the Gullah coast as one of the nation's eleven most endangered historical sites (Tibbetts, 11). Gullah festivals, institutes, conferences, and even operas woo tens of thousands yearly. And a maturing generation of Nick Jr. TV-viewers world-wide, along with their parents and guardians, regularly mimic my wife Natalie and me, singing a playful line from our award-winning show's theme song – "Let's all go to Gullah Gullah Island." Whereas *Gullah Gullah Island* is imaginary, Gullah culture really exists. And others are echoing the sentiments stated by Congressman Clyburn: "The Gullah/Geechee culture is the last vestige of fusion of African and European languages and traditions brought to these coastal areas. I cannot sit idly by and watch an entire culture disappear that represents my heritage and the heritage of those who look like me" (Derrick, Hope. Clyburn (SC06) – Press Release).

My own personal awareness and appreciation of Gullah culture has grown since the 1986 publication of this book's forerunner, *Reminiscences of Sea Island Heritage, Legacy of Freedmen on St. Helena Island*. In the preface, I cited the book as:

> ". . . an aesthetic documentation of the lifestyles, customs, super-
> stitions and lore of the St. Helena Island people, which soon may

be altogether forgotten. As condominiums and resort communities become as commonplace as the Spanish moss draping aged oaks, and as third and fourth generation Islanders cease to identify with a heritage dear to their forbears, that heritage is being hushed and stilled. This work is a time capsule, presented with Sea Island flavoring. It is a people's story of how they 'got over,' by surviving the hard times, and how and what they learned about life." (Daise 1986)

At that time, "Gullah" was a term used more readily by scholars, linguists, and academicians. "Geechee" was used as an invective or insult. "Sea Island heritage," however, had become a term of endearment and ownership.

Gullah Branches, West African Roots documents what I've learned about my heritage. Following the publication of its prequel, my wife Natalie and I packaged its oral histories, songs, stories, and historical photographs into a multimedia theatrical performance entitled "Sea Island Montage."

I recall eyeing an elementary school student as we began a performance during the late 1980s. She turned completely around in her rotating, cafeteria-table seat, closed her eyes, and covered her ears. The images were ugly, she confided to her teacher later. She didn't want to hear the songs or listen to the stories because she was unaccustomed to positive presentations that related to her cultural identity. I've learned that many Gullah people hate being Gullah.

After a performance for a national conference some years ago, a viewer sought us out as we left the stage. An element of one our stories had given her an *Aha!* moment. Hearing the Gullah belief that one should not comb his or her hair outdoors because a bird could make a nest with that hair and the individual would then get headaches had caught her attention. She was from California, she said, complaining that her live-in mother-in-law, who was from a South Carolina sea island, kept bagsful of hair about the house. Until our performance, she had written her mother-in-law off as simple-minded, weird, and wacky. I've learned that many people don't understand Gullah ways.

I've spoken Gullah during performances and watched the responses of those who have sat with an air of academic dignity but who, nonetheless, surprised themselves with how readily they understood a Gullah word or expression. I've learned that lots of people who may not have wanted to identify with being Gullah really are.

On the other spectrum, I've been questioned by white Americans whose family members were raised in isolated sea island communities in which African descendants greatly outnumbered whites. Their family members speak Gullah, practice Gullah beliefs and traditions, and respect the culture, they've told me. "Are they not Gullah or of Gullah heritage?" many have asked. Their questioning has ensued unanswered while, on another note, *beenyahs*, or native islanders, have argued vehemently that *comeyahs*, or transplants to Gullah communities, are not and never will be Gullah. I've learned that Gullah ownership, for some, is a conundrum.

As the marsh grass grows, some cultural enthusiasts have indoctrinated others with beliefs that Gullah people live in shacks only . . . or sing only plantation ditties . . . or dress only in antebellum or regal West African apparel . . . or work only as farmers, shrimpers, oystermen, sweetgrass basket makers, or craftsmen and women . . . or should not consider identifying with Gullah heritage unless they can document it unequivocally.

My "Gullah/Geechee Rhythms" PowerPoint presentation cites ten memorable cultural touchstones that readily identify the heritage. I use the tune of "Children, Go Where I Send Thee," a coded message song sung by Harriet Tubman as she led hundreds along the Underground Railroad, to declare, "Dats Right, I Am a Gullah." The song's concluding lyrics state, "I'm Gullah cause my ancestas [*sic*] came from West Africa."

Many African Americans, I'm aware, are stumped about how to research their ancestry. In July 2006, I learned from DNA testing through the National Geographic Society's "The Genographic Project" that my deep ancestral history, with genetic markers reaching back about 60,000 years, is from sub-Saharan Africa (www.nationalgeographic.com/genographic). My DNA report states:

> You are descended from an ancient African lineage. In North Africa, this haplogroup (E3a) is found at frequencies of five to 10 percent among Berbers, Tunisians, and Moroccan Arabs. Because it is also predominant in West Africa, many African-Americans also trace their genetic history to this line of descent.
>
> The man who gave rise to your first genetic marker in your lineage probably lived in northeast Africa in the region of the Rift Valley, perhaps in present-day Ethiopia, Kenya, or Tanzania, some 31,000 to 79,000 years ago. Scientists put the most likely date for

when he lived at around 50,000 years ago. His descendants became the only lineage to survive outside of Africa, making him the common ancestor of every non-African man living today.

Longing to know my ancestral legacy from the period of the Transatlantic Slave Trade, however, I pursued subsequent DNA testing through African Ancestry, Inc. (www.africanancestry.com). I, like many African Americans, yearned to trace my heritage to a particular African country or village or clan, where the genetic markers are evident in body language, physical features, and spiritual connection.

My sixteen-year-old grand-nephew, Kendall Session, of Sumter, South Carolina, found this link when visiting Kenya on a missionary trip with his father Ernest during the summer of 2006.

"They told me I looked like them!" Kendall said with excitement. "They'd tell me that maybe my family's ancestors had come from Kenya to America to work as slaves. They said my facial features, especially my eyes, looked like theirs. And, yes, my eyes do resemble theirs. And I saw baskets like the ones I see on the islands of South Carolina. And the songs they sang—the rhythms and the harmonies—were like the ones sung on the islands. I felt like, yeah, maybe they really are my people!"

Kendall is the son of my oldest niece, Marva Carr Session, who is the oldest child of my eldest sibling. Interestingly, other nieces and nephews have told me that they're often asked if they're Kenyan.

I received my DNA report from African Ancestry, Inc., on Saturday, September 14, and opened the envelope slowly, with nervous anticipation. I'd felt at home when I'd visited Ghana and Sierra Leone, but just where were my people really from?

"The mitochondrial DNA (maternal) sequence that we determined from your sample shares ancestry with the Temne people in Sierra Leone today," the report read. "The Y chromosome DNA markers (paternal) that we determined from your sample share ancestry with the Ewe and Akan people in Ghana today."

"So, Daddy," my daughter Sara proclaimed about the results, "you had a family reunion each time you went to Africa and didn't even know it, huh?"

I've learned that being Gullah has become highly esteemed. Such was the opinion of the nearly 2,500 persons gathered for the day-long celebration of the release of *De Nyew Testament*, or Gullah Bible, by the American Bible Society. Ardell Greene, one of the charter members of the Sea Island Translation Team of St. Helena Island, South Carolina, which worked in cooperation with Wycliffe Bible Translators, spoke during the festivities at JAARS in Waxhaw, North Carolina, on November 5, 2005.

"In 1979, my husband and I were asked to help to do a Bible in Gullah," she stated. Her husband, Ervin Greene, was pastor of historic Brick Baptist Church on St. Helena Island. "At that time if people asked if I was Gullah, I would say, `No, I am not Gullah!' We told Pat and Claude Sharpe [the Wycliffe Bible consultants], no, we would not help with the project because the educators have said that Gullah should not be spoken.

"But I've grown in [respect for] Gullah," she said in summary of her twenty-six-year work toward translating the *New Testament*. "As we began to translate, I became very excited. When I read Gullah scripture to others now, they get excited, sometimes expressing that feeling in laughter. They can identify with it.

"People used to ask, `Are you Gullah?' and I would say, `No, I'm not!' But now I say, `Yeah, A Gullah! A Gullah down!'"

Like Ardell Greene, many have shed shame and embarrassment about Gullah culture and are happy to identify themselves as "Gullah down!"—that is, being truly, authentically, and proudly Gullah.

I've learned, most importantly, from first-hand experience and observation that Gullah and Geechee customs are carryovers of West African heritage. Until I visited West African countries, I had recounted that statement because I had read it and believed it. But now I know!

In 2004 I participated in a five-week U.S. Department of Education Fulbright-Hays "Teaching and Learning in Ghana Program," administered through Charleston Southern University. My first trip to the Motherland inspired me to write a song, "Nshira Nka Mikra," which in Fante means "My soul has been blessed!" Translated in Gullah, that's "My soul been bless!" I saw the links in cultures. I was moved and exhilarated and wrote poetry and short stories and journal entries to tell others about all that I had experienced!

In May 2005 I was asked by anthropologist, historian, and professor Joseph Opala, of James Madison University, to serve as Gullah ambassador during "Priscilla's Homecoming" in Sierra Leone. The historic one-week celebration was a Gullah homecoming for Thomalind Martin Polite of Charleston, South

Carolina. In 1756, her great-great-great-great-great-grandmother, at the age of ten, was kidnapped in Sierra Leone, boarded on the Rhode Island slave ship *Hare*, and brought to a rice plantation in South Carolina. Planter Elias Ball II purchased her and gave her the name Priscilla. Through "Priscilla's Homecoming," the Martin family connected with the country of its ancestral legacy.

The event was unprecedented because Martin family members possessed written documentation to connect their past. These came from the Ball family slave records and museum records from the *Hare*. I, too, made connections throughout my participation in this one-of-a-kind, almost-too-phenomenal-to-be-real, historic event. I recalled the tunes of Gullah spirituals and folksongs and used them to chronicle my daily experiences. As part of the "Gullah/Geechee Program Series" at Brookgreen Gardens, in Murrells Inlet, South Carolina, where I work as Vice President for Creative Education, and in continuation of its promotion of Gullah history, I've shared these songs and information with visitors from around the country.

Reflecting my zeal from my two African sojourns, *Gullah Branches, West African Roots* is an aesthetic documentation of the lifestyles, customs, superstitions, and lore of cultures from which Gullahs and Geechees sprang. It is a collection of writings that identify a heritage closely related to other cultures of the African Diaspora. This work is a time capsule, presented with sea island flavoring. Its stories and songs showcase that, indeed, there is a connection! Those who may not be able to witness this connection firsthand can—without doubt—believe, cherish, celebrate!

"There's A Connection"

(Sung to the tune of Gullah spiritual "I Don't Mind")

Africa. West Africa.
Africa. West Africa.
There's a connection deep down in my spirit
With Africa. West Africa.

I've been to Ghana and Sierra Leone.
I walked down the streets and felt right at home.
There's a connection deep down in my spirit
With Africa. West Africa.

I looked into dark faces everywhere I'd go.
Something behind their eyes let me know
There's a connection deep down in my spirit
With Africa. West Africa.

Africa. West Africa.
Africa. West Africa.
There's a connection deep down in my spirit
With Africa. West Africa.

I'd hear the music, then start to dance.
Africans would look at me and say, "A undastan…"
There's a connection deep down in my spirit
With Africa. West Africa.

In slave castles, I'd hear the groans
Of ancestors moaning, "We are one!"
There's a connection deep down in my spirit
With Africa. West Africa.

Africa. West Africa.
Africa. West Africa.
There's a connection deep down in my spirit
With Africa. West Africa.

Words by Ronald Daise
© 2005

TABLE OF CONTENTS

SECTION 7 .... *160*
Africa. West Africa.
Africa. West Africa.
There's a connection deep down in my spirit
With Africa. West Africa.

Gullah Branches, West African Roots

Africa. West Africa.
Africa. West Africa.
There's a connection deep down in my spirit
With Africa. West Africa.

Hush! Hush! Somebody callin my name!

In August 2004, following my first visit to West Africa, I began working at Brookgreen Gardens, in Murrell's Inlet, South Carolina. As Vice President for Creative Education, I inherited an initiative to promote the Gullah culture of Brookgreen Gardens, in particular, and the surrounding communities of the Lowcountry, in general. Brookgreen, the country's premier sculpture gardens, was established in 1931 by philanthropist Archer Huntington and his wife, sculptor Anna Hyatt Huntington. The couple purchased 9,100 acres, four abandoned rice plantations—Brookgreen, The Oaks, Springfield, and Laurel Hill—to showcase Anna Hyatt Huntington's works as well as those of her friends. A National Historic Landmark, Brookgreen Gardens is "Ever Changing. Simply Amazing." not only because of its imaginative and impeccable sculptures, verdant gardens, and zoo of animals native to the southeast and domestic animals of the plantation era but also because of its rich Gullah history. Several of the African-American staff members are descendants of workers at Brookgreen Plantation.

From my office window, I overlook Brookgreen Main, Brookgreen Plantation's major ricefield, which teemed with enslaved African workers some 200 years ago. I see glimpses of them from time to time. As I walk The Lowcountry Trail—amidst ancient live oaks draped with moss and archeological depictions of the overseer's cabin, smokehouse, kitchen, and dependency—I sense the presence of their spirits. I hear their voices, too: "Bout time oona come," they whisper. "Tell de wol bout we. Tell dem bout all we done done. All we come shru. You yeddy me?"

To honor their memories, I premiered my one-man production of "My Soul Been Bless! Gullah Roots, Branches, Blossoms" in the Wall Lowcountry Center Auditorium on my forty-ninth birthday. My reader's theater renditions of stories about Ghana's slave dungeons, ties to Gullah culture, and scenic beauty moved audience members, which included a record number of African-Americans. As I walked to my car afterward, rain drizzled and misted, like the tears of Elders. Tears of joy? I wondered. Tears of pride?

Within a few weeks of the premier, I was invited to serve as Gullah ambassador for "Priscilla's Homecoming" in Sierra Leone, West Africa. This Gullah homecoming connected the family of Thomalind Martin Polite of Charleston, South Carolina, with the country of its matriarch, Priscilla, who had been enslaved in 1756, at the age of ten.

While in Sierra Leone, I peered into the eyes of people around me and wondered if they could be related to enslaved Africans who, centuries ago, had worked at Brookgreen Plantation. During the slave era, forty-three percent of Africans in South Carolina had come from the Rice Coast. My journey there reinforced my awareness of the close connection of today's Gullah people with their West African ancestors.

Others also may sense a connection or strain for an understanding of historical and cultural context as they meander down Brookgreen Gardens's Lowcountry Trail.

Visitors learn from the introductory panel:

> One-quarter mile in length, the Lowcountry Trail crosses the hillside overlooking Mainfield, a Brookgreen rice field. For enslaved Africans on Brookgreen, this hill was a bridge between the world of daily work and the familiarity of life in Slave Village beyond the crest of the hill. The rhythms of life—planting, growing, harvesting, threshing—changed seasonally for everyone on the rice plantation.
>
> Archeological projects have revealed the remains of four structures on the hillside: the site of the overseer's residence at the apex of the hill, and its kitchen, smokehouse and dependency closer to the edge of the rice field. Along the trail, four stainless steel figures have been placed to represent the Plantation Owner, the Overseer, and an enslaved African Male and Female. They provide reminders of plantation life and the associated joys and sadness of the human experience played out here nearly 200 years ago. (Daise 2005)

Sculptor Babette Bloch stated, "As I read and researched and worked on the drawings, I knew I wanted each work to tell the stories. The stories are rich! I envision the Lowcountry Trail as building a bridge—a bridge of hope, of healing. I see it as a place of contemplation, for understanding, and even as a place for celebrating the Gullah cultural heritage."

True to Babette Bloch's vision, as I walk the Lowcountry Trail, I sense a flow that parallels the rhythm of life I witnessed in Sierra Leone. I saw adults pounding mortars and pestles, as were used at Brookgreen Plantation centuries ago. I watched families in villages cooking, conversing, playing games, washing clothes in their yards, or coming out of small domiciles that seemingly thrived with life and respect for life. I heard conversations in Krio, the *lingua franca* of Sierra Leone, which sounds remarkably like Gullah spoken yesteryear and today. I walked through the ruins of Bunce Island, the slave prison from which thousands upon thousands of West Africans last saw their homeland before beginning the arduous journey known as the Middle Passage. For many, the final leg journey, upon reaching the New World, took them to rice plantations in South Carolina and Georgia.

More indelibly, I heard the shouts and witnessed the looks of appreciation and honor given to "di Priscilla uman," as some called Thomalind Martin Polite. From statesmen to villagers, all wanted to regale and glimpse her—a descendant of a family member who had left in chains, who had returned, who had bridged a connection. (Daise 2005)

For Gullah and Geechee descendants and other African-Americans who stroll the Brookgreen Gardens Lowcountry Trail, the experience will tap many sensibilities. It will be a rhythmic song, a heaping serving of flavorful rice, a strange but familiar speechway, and a spiritual journey—all in one. Gullah music, foods, language, and beliefs are ways in which our heritage continues to impact the American cultural landscape. When Gullah descendants—and those of other cultures—visit this site, these metaphors of experience will pervade and enrich them.

Many will find themselves filled with questions, resolutions, and meditations. One Gullah belief, based in West African heritage, is that the ancestors remain nearby—guiding, reproving, helping. Many living persons, as they wind their way along the trail, may hear stories unfold by voices that have been hushed for centuries, voices that shout for their stories to be heard! Some may even hear voices calling their names.

A Gullah Journey Along "The Lowcountry Trail" at Brookgreen Gardens

I created the following fictionalized story as part of an audio tour script for The Lowcountry Trail. It is set at Brookgreen Plantation in 1807, the year before the Transatlantic Slave Trade was abolished. The names of the characters are actual names of enslaved Africans at Brookgreen, circa 1831–1850. They are found in the medical records of Dr. Andrew Hasell, who served as primary physician for the region, including Sandy Island and the Plantersville area. Used by permission of Bob Jewell, president and CEO, Brookgreen Gardens.

Stainless steel, laser-cut sculptures by Babette Bloch along The Lowcountry Trail depict four characters who helped in the development of Gullah culture on rice plantations of South Carolina and Georgia: Plantation Owner (right), Overseer, Enslaved African Male, and Enslaved African Female. Courtesy, Brookgreen Gardens, a National Historic Landmark. Photos by author.

It's early morning, the time of day known in Slave Village as *dayclean*. Planter John Joshua Ward is away from Brookgreen Plantation. Wealthy and politically powerful, he has journeyed to Charleston and will return tomorrow. In his presence or absence, however, the plantation work continues with efficiency—daily, weekly, monthly, and seasonally.

Planter Ward's opinions are sought after by governmental officials, and his family's social status is respected by many. He has purchased land, hundreds of African captives, farm tools, food, clothes, and machinery and has hired an overseer. This land and these rice fields are a major investment! They are among 45,000 acres of rice fields in Georgetown County. Surrounding plantations may flounder, he reasons, but not his. Brookgreen Plantation will succeed! It is his life.

If Planter Ward had not been traveling, young Congo Jim would have attempted to bring the news to him directly. The news is this: one of Master Ward's favorite slaves is dying. Is it Tom, the coachman? Couldn't be. Mr. Ward would be aware of this, as Tom is with him now, out of town. How about Nippy, the nurse? Maybe it's Sarah, the cook? The mystery will unravel before this plantation day ends. Perhaps the dying slave is Ben, the trunkminder.

In Slave Village, the sense of approaching death has been a tangible feeling throughout the night inside the cabins of the nearly 500 enslaved Africans. Pained screaming in the dying slave's solitary cabin did not begin until after midnight, or, rather, *hag-hollerin time*. The acute spasms had startled the slave and surprised all family members as well as neighbors, as conditions worsened during the night. Cuffey, the aged slave brought from the African Grain Coast, had predicted the death, telling everyone that a white bird had flown into the cabin of the dying slave yesterday and did not leave until all workers had returned home. It was a sure sign, he decreed, that death was a-comin'—and a-comin' quickly!

In Master Ward's absence, Congo Jim has come early to the overseer's cottage. Overseer Joe Pinckney is startled to hear the knock at his back door, even before he has risen to review his journal. But the voice calling his name is a familiar one. In fact, Joe Pinckney knows the voices, capabilities, temperaments, and habits of all the enslaved workers on the plantation—young and old, male and female. He assigns them their daily tasks and records their productivity in his trusted journal, or notebook, in order to ensure Master Ward

Overseer.

that he is managing well the day-to-day operations of Brookgreen Plantation.

Joe Pinckney listens to Congo Jim's story about a sick slave. Then Pinckney sends him on his way before informing him to report to Mainfield when the horn blows. He tells him to bring the hoe—to not be late.

"Death is a part of life," Pinckney reasons to himself. "A slave dies; a new slave is purchased. Master Ward, upon his return, will take care of any transitions of life.

Whether slaves are old or newly purchased, Ward will feed them, clothe them, house them, work them. Life will go on.

"Besides," Pinckney reasons, "today's picture can't be as abysmal as Congo Jim has described it. There was no unusual activity surrounding the slave in question yesterday." The overseer checks his journal. The slave's task had been completed. . . . Early. As always. . . . A good slave.

Before leaving the backyard and turning to re-enter his home, Pinckney makes a mental note that if news of this sickness worsens throughout the day, he will send young Absolom to fetch Dr. Hasell from his office on Waccamaw Neck. And, Congo Jim, he further notes, might very well one day advance to a higher station. Maybe he could become a driver . . . yes, a driver —a slave who's respected and feared by all other slaves on the plantation.

Pinckney has worked as overseer on a few other plantations before Brookgreen. Being second-in-command to a prosperous planter is a position that makes his life meaningful.

He realizes there is something about the teenage slave named Congo Jim, who looks and works like someone beyond his age. Plantation life and Congo Jim seem like a good fit. He will be sure to tell Planter Ward, upon his return, about Congo Jim's actions.

"Deat a part ob life," the enslaved workers spend their day thinking. *"Wheneba a slabe die, a new slabe git purchase. An life jus gone on."* In English: Death is a part of life. A slave dies, a new slave is purchased. Life goes on.

The enslaved workers have toiled from early morning, or *fus whistle blow*—the time when Gabriel, the driver, blows into a conch shell to call the slaves to work— until *high nyoon*. It is now time to rest briefly and eat lunch. Some have sung songs silently as they've worked in the fields or washed clothese or made bricks or pounded mortars and pestles for rice to cook at dinnertime.

Today is different for many of them. A *crossin ova*, or transition from life to death, is soon to come. They each know that the full weight of their feelings cannot immobilize them, however. They must continue. If they don't, then *Driva* Gabriel might lash them. Overseer Pinckney would see to that.

The thought of death makes Sukey think of home. Not in Slave Village, where she has lived for only a year. Home—back in Africa. She remembers using mortars and pestles with her mother in her rice village. She wonders if she'll ever see her mother or father or other relatives again. Sukey wants to cry. Instead, she holds her head high. Life goes on. *She* must go on. She remembers Sierra Leonean funeral celebrations where rice was cooked and mashed with other ingredients and placed on the deceased member's grave. To Sukey, rice is sacred. Rice is used to bid farewell to the living and to welcome them into the world of a family's ancestors.

"Life jus gone on," she thinks to herself. She plans to bring pride to her family, to her ancestors as she works in these rice fields. Even though these are not the rice fields of her family or of villagers from her youth, she *must* go on.

Sarah, the cook, has thought about death while preparing the overseer's breakfast and now lunch. For the midday meal, she serves rice bird stew over rice and turnip greens with roots. For the Pinckneys' family dinner, she will prepare smothered pork chops, rice, collard greens, and cornbread with molasses.

When she goes to the smokehouse, Sarah cuts an extra piece of

Enslaved African Female.

pork fatback and stuffs it into her apron pocket. She plots as she works. That evening, she will carry it over to that solitary cabin for her extended family member in Slave Row. Sarah's sister, Nippy, had spoken to her on the way to her task of flailing the rice plants. She had said that the sick slave's pain was on his right side and that she had brewed some leaves from the life-everlasting plant for tea.

Nippy is called nurse by some and root doctor by others because she knows what roots or berries or leaves to gather and boil, or crush, or steep for medical ailments. Sarah will bring Nippy the salted fatback to lay on the death-bound slave's belly, to the right of his belly button, to draw out infection.

"Deat a part ob life," Sarah tells herself as she seasons, boils, and bakes foods to sustain the life of the overseer's family. *"Wheneba a slabe die, a new slabe git purchase. An life jus gone on."*

Stealing the piece of pork meat from the smokehouse will allow her to do something to sustain the life of someone whose features resemble hers, Sarah convinces herself. The thought of another slave dying slices her emotions sharply like a butcher knife chopping stalks of collards. She wonders if she can continue to go on. Death could soon come looking for her, too, she realizes, and she would leave this world as a cook on Brookgreen Plantation. This had not been her dream. How long would life go on?

Each time Congo Jim walks past the cabin of Sarah and her husband, something inside him recoils. And, today, Overseer Pinckney has assigned him to hoe the field beside their cabin. His task is not yet complete and late afternoon, or *sun way lay over*, is quickly approaching. On other days, his work would have long ago been finished.

Congo Jim knows that the cook and driver's cabin looks just like the others in Slave Village, just like the one he sleeps in, but this one is close to the overseer's house and stands apart from the others all huddled together across the crest of the hill. The distinction irritates him whenever he looks at it. He wonders if Sarah and Tom would rather live in Slave Village. He is horrified to think that some slaves are made to stay apart from others.

Inside, Congo Jim is seething. On the outside, though, his face seems serene. Since leaving Africa, he has learned to mask his feelings, especially the ones that make his nostrils flare, his eyes widen, and his speech quicken. Such honesty, clothed in *his* skin color, would bring trouble, Ben the trunkminder had taught him since his arrival.

Knowing about Ben's sudden sickness throughout the night and hearing about Cuffey's death watch has slowed Jim's progress today. Ben, strong and caring, has been like a father to Jim. Every boy needs a father—especially when in a new land.

Jim had wanted to be called by his African name. "Why do they call me Congo Jim?" he had cried to Ben. "I am not from Congo. I am from Ibo land. My name is Akin [pronounced AH-keen]. Akin means 'courage is worthy of a crown.' What does this name Jim mean? How can I show any kind of courage?"

Ben had convinced him to remember his African name but to use the name Jim that Master Ward had given him.

Jim wants to wed a Nigerian Ibo girl living on a plantation on nearby Sandy Island. He is willling to "work-out," away from Brookgreen Plantation, after he's finished his daily tasks in order to labor as a carpenter so that he can earn wages to pay whatever price her owner and his owner require. But Planter Ward has planned that Jim will marry Sukey. They and their children will continue to live on Brookgreen Plantation.

"*Deat a part ob life*," Jim grunts as he heads back to Slave Row. "*Wheneba a slabe die, a new slabe git purchase. An life jus gone on.*"

Over the horizon, the sun has fallen into the river. The time is now *sundong* and Ben the trunkminder has died of acute appendicitis. Absolom was sent to secure Dr. Hasell, but the physi-

Enslaved African Male.

cian did not arrive before the dying slave's inflamed organ ruptured.

Just as the yearly arrival of bobolinks, or rice birds, brings destruction to the rice plants, the arrival of a white bird perched inside a slave cabin has been a sign of the death of a slave on Brookgreen Plantation. When Planter Ward returns the next day, Ben's funeral is held at *blaack daak*, the time when you can't see your hand in front of your face. Slave funerals are held at nighttime, not to interfere with the daily production of rice.

"Ben was trustworthy . . . and . . . and reliable," Master Ward states as he stands beside his wife in Slave Village. "He wasn't born here, but Ben knew this plantation. And he knew these rice fields better than I know some members of my own family. He grew up here at Brookgreen. Minding the rice—raising and lowering the trunks to flood and drain these fields—was his life! Death is a part of life, but Ben will be sadly missed."

After the Wards returned to their home, mourners mourned. Singers sang. Ben's youngest grandchild was passed once back and forth over the open grave to protect the child from being snatched prematurely into the spirit world. Family and friends placed Ben's pipe, a broken glass bottle, and conch shells atop his grave in Slave Cemetery. They made sure the grave had been dug the night before so that the sun would have been able to set on the open grave before the burial. That way, it was believed, his soul would be at peace.

Mourners reminisced about how Ben would smoke his pipe each evening in Slave Village and tell stories to his grandchildren gathered around his knees. He'd tell them that there was a better place somewhere. Then, for clarity, his baritone voice would boom, "*You yeddy me?*"

Brookgreen Plantation paused with respectfulness. As the wind rustled over the open tops of colorful bottles hanging upside down on Bottle Trees, captive evil spirits shrieked and howled. Those who discounted old African beliefs glanced about with a surreptitious eye and snickered shamelessly; then they looked away in haste.

The rhythms of life began again and continued—planting, growing, harvesting, threshing . . . .

Rice field.

Come on een de room. . . . He gib me all my medicine een de praya room!

Gullah culture's rootedness in spirituality, as handed down by the culture of West African forebears and the need of Gullah people to hear the word of God in their own language, were themes exhorted during the American Bible Society's celebration of the release of *De Nyew Testament* at JAARS, in Waxhaw, North Carolina, on November 5, 2005. The Gullah *New Testament* translation was completed by the Sea Island Translation Team of St. Helena Island, South Carolina, in cooperation with Wycliffe Bible Translators.

With exceeding joy, I emceed the JAARS "Gullah *New Testament* Celebration" dedicatory program! I greeted an enthusiastic group of about 1,400 with these words:

> When I've presented the Christmas story in Gullah from *De Good Nyews Bout Jedus Christ Wa Luke Write* and when I've presented other scriptures in Gullah, I've observed numerous responses. Many have laughed, but not with the laughter of derision. The laughter—sometimes belly-deep, sometimes as gasps and chuckles—has been an affirmation of understanding what has been spoken.
>
> Some audience members have listened silently and with a forbearance that has mirrored some inner pain. "I used to speak that way," an elder woman confided afterward. "I can't now," she added. "I had it beaten out of me!"
>
> Most often, however, the eyes of listeners have been bright. They have been radiant with the light of God, whose Word—in all languages—lights our footsteps and guides our way.
>
> I'm honored to have been one of the charter members of The Sea Island Translation Team and Literacy Project. I participated as

a newlywed with my wife Natalie and with my mother, Kathleen G. Daise, who last Tuesday turned ninety-two years old. My mother, a former school teacher and a 1933 graduate of Penn School, joined the endeavor because it was about making the Word of God *plain* to others, even though speaking Gullah had been discouraged in our home. Throughout most of her life, Gullah had been regarded as broken English.

My wife's interest blossomed after she heard a passage and thought about how her great-grandmother, Sarah Jackson—who always clutched her Bible but who couldn't read or write—would have received hearing the translation with gladness! She assisted by videotaping presentations and meetings.

I assisted the team by making public presentations of scriptures in Gullah because Gullah is my heritage and doing God's will is my charge. With respect to Wycliffe workers Pat and Claude Sharpe, team members who began—and team members who endured—we all can say today in the words of the old spiritual, "Good Lawd, A done done. A done done what you tol me ta do!"

Dr. Emory Campbell, Executive Director Emeritus of Penn Center and a charter Sea Island Translation Team member, extolled the Wycliffe Bible Translators' family of organizations. "You stuck with us because you thought the culture was of value," he said. "The values of family and spirituality will sustain the culture."

De Nyew Testament, or Gullah Bible, was released at JAARS in Waxhaw, North Carolina, on November 5, 2005, and one week later at the Penn Center Heritage Days festival on St. Helena Island, South Carolina.
Courtesy, JAARS, Inc., Waxhaw, North Carolina.

Ron, charter member of the Sea Island Translation Team that began translating the Bible into Sea Island Creole, also known as Gullah, addresses an audience of about 1,400 gathered at JAARS for the Gullah New Testament Celebration dedicatory program.
Courtesy, JAARS, Inc.

Campbell said his initial response to learning about an interest in translating a Gullah Bible was that it was just another thing to discount Black people. "Man, you betta git way from heh," he said he told the Sharpes. "Dere's no such ting as Gullah! But when they showed me Gullah words and expressions with West African roots, I was convinced!"

Campbell concluded his address during the dedication ceremony with comparing the Gullah translation workers to a civil rights icon who had recently been memorialized. "Like Rosa Parks, this team has freed us," he stated. "They have set us free because they have given us the Word of God!"

Ken Schmitt, Americas Area Director of Summer Institute of Linguistics (SIL), International, echoed Campbell's thoughts. "The Word of God is eternal, creative, powerful, life-giving, light-bringing, darkness-shattering," he said. "But the most astounding fact is that `the word became flesh and dwelt among us. And we beheld His glory, the glory of the only begotten of the Father, full of grace and truth.' Until the Word became incarnate, entered our culture, spoke our language, we were unable to fully see God's glory, to apprehend grace and truth. What we celebrate today is the incarnation of the Word into the Gullah culture through the Gullah language. What John described in the first century is being reenacted in the 21st century. The eternal, creative, life-giving, light-bringing, darkness-shattering Word of God has pitched its tent at the center of the Gullah culture so that the Gullah can behold the glory of the only begotten of the Father and learn of His grace and truth in a language that speaks to their hearts."

Frank Murray of De Gullah Singers, a five-member family performance group from Wadmalaw Island, South Carolina, told audience members that

Gullah people sang songs and melodies that brought their ancestors through the tribulations of slavery. "When they weren't allowed in the churches, they would go into the woods, in the bush arbors to praise God," he explained.

De Gullah Singers—accompanying themselves with a washboard and copper tubing on fingers, a cowbell and stick, a tambourine, and an oak branch that pounded the floor—performed hand-clapping, foot-thumping praise house songs to West African rhythms that had been handed down from centuries ago and that still resound today.

> Come on een de room.
> Come on een de room.
> Jedus is my docta
> An He write up all my scription
> An He gib me all my medicine
> Een de praya room!

Their song was an acclamation that many Gullah people have long known the power and the presence of God. Linguistics consultant for SIL International and a Sea Island Translation Team member, David Frank brought the *New Testament* Project to completion following the death of Pat Sharpe. He called the Gullah Translation Team charter members and translators onstage and to everyone's surprise unwrapped a package. When translator Vernetta Canteen received a copy of *De Nyew Testament*, she grasped it to her bosom, closed her eyes, and bowed her head. Other members smiled widely and looked at the Bible with wonder and bright eyes.

My wife Natalie responded with a shudder and gasp and brushed away teardrops. "The ceremony made me realize that some things that may have started a long time ago, that may have only moved forward in small increments over time still have value," she said.

When Natalie joined the team, she had recently moved to Beaufort from Syracuse, New York. "This Bible project was a catalyst," she stated. "Since its start, so much has happened. We've moved toward acceptance of the language by Gullahs as well as by the international community. And language is just a piece of what this document means. It's the Bible. And the Bible means so much! Sometimes you may think what you're doing is so small, so insignificant, but if you don't give up, if you don't get weary, you'll see the value one day."

Her thoughts paralleled the sentiments conveyed in the lyrics of another song performed by De Gullah Singers. The words also celebrated the resilience, the fortitude, the faith of a people:

A been walkin a road a long time . . .
A been prayin a praya a long time . . .
A been singin a song a long time . . .
An A ent got weary yet!

Sea Island Translation Team members respond with emotion after David Frank, far right, awards them copies of the Gullah Bible. Left to right: Ardell Green, Vernetta Canteen, Natalie Daise, Ron, and Emory Campbell (second from right). Campbell's wife Emma, third from right, is also pictured. Courtesy, JAARS, Inc.

Een de midnight ouah, de Lord is nigh. . . .

On November 11, 2005, during the Penn Center Heritage Days Festival on St. Helena Island, South Carolina, the Gullah Bible debuted in the heart of the Gullah community. Its unveiling reinforced and highlighted the festival theme: Preserving Gullah Traditions and Culture through Language.

"I think we have done a good job throughout the years in preserving our culture through stories and songs," said St. Helena Island resident Alfreda Thompson. "But now, an even more exciting part of our culture, our language, is in writing. When you have something you can pick up and read, you can always go back to it from generation to generation. That's one reason why this Gullah Bible is so important!"

Thompson, who joined the Sea Island Translation Team in 1991, said the weekend's launch of the Bible had been a very emotional experience. "I don't know why He chose us!" she stated. "But God chose a people like us—the Gullah people—to bring about this project for the country, for the world. This is God's doing. Each time we came to a pause in the work, God raised someone up to complete it. And it has gained nationwide attention. . . . I don't know why God chose us! But God is doing something. He's always at work. And He's always doing something."

Elmer and Ruth Ash, Gullah *New Testament* representatives and distributors, reported selling an estimated 1,500 copies of *De Nyew Testament* during the three-day festival, which was attended by about 15,000. Ten thousand copies were printed by the American Bible Society.

Presenters discussed the following topics throughout the festival's symposium:

- Preserving the Cultural Links of Language
- Using Language to Preserve Our Culture
- Using Language to Link Back to Africa

David Frank, Linguistics Consultant for Summer Institute of Linguistics (SIL), International, and Sea Island Translation Team translators Vernetta Canteen and Ardell Greene conduct a demonstration of the translation process during the 2005 Penn Center Heritage Days festival.
Courtesy, JAARS, Inc.

- Using Language to Advance Our Culture: The Bible Translation Project
- Using Quilts to Talk about Heritage & Culture: Musical Demonstration

"This Bible doesn't validate Gullah as a language," said David Frank, linguistics consultant for SIL International and a Sea Island Translation Team member. "It [Gullah] always was a language. Now we can read it together. And learn from it together."

De Nyew Testament includes marginal text of the King James version. Several English Bible translations, however, were used for reference in the translation process. As stated in the preface, "The spelling used in the Gullah *New Testament* is a practical orthography. It is not ideal in all respects, but this spelling of Gullah words is designed for Gullah speakers who are already literate in English . . . and would not be optimal for someone who does not already know how to read English, nor for someone who does not know how to speak Gullah. The spelling of Gullah is based on English, but that should not be taken to mean that Gullah is a dialect of English, despite obvious similarities. English has had its influence on Gullah, both in its origin as an English creole and in its development over the years. But Gullah, too, has had more of an influence on English than many people realize. . . . The goal has been to make a translation from the original language into Gullah that is clear in meaning, accurate, and natural in its expression." (*De Nyew Testament* 2005)

Frank addressed the tedious translation process of evaluating and revising passages, then re-evaluating and re-revising. "The translation will stand up to the scrutiny of scholars," he stated, "but the church will be the target audience for this new translation. It will mean that preachers will not have to make up translations into Gullah on the spot, and the translations will not be different each time. . . . Rev. Ervin Greene [former project director] told me of a man who had heard him recite a translation from *De Good Nyews Wa Luke Write* and had said to him, `Reb, dat de fus time A heh God taak de same way A taak!'" (Lightbody 2005)

The importance of this phenomenon was echoed by presenter Joseph Opala, an historian who lived in Sierra Leone for seventeen years. Renowned for his research on "the Gullah connection," the historical thread that links the people of Sierra Leone to the Gullah people of South Carolina and Georgia, Opala discussed his 1998 documentary film *The Language You Cry In*. The project was so named, he said, following an aged African chief's succinct explanation about why an enslaved African woman in coastal Georgia during the 1700s would remember a Mende funeral song and share it with her children. The song has endured within the family of Amelia Dawley of Harris Neck, Georgia, for generations.

Opala recounted, "The chief said, 'That song was the one thing that would connect her with her family, with her home because it had been sung when all her relatives had died.' Then the chief told us a proverb: `You know a person's true identity by the language they cry in.' I didn't fully understand at first. Then he explained, `When you're in sorrow or when you're in pain, you will always cry out in your mother tongue.'"

Mary Moran, who remembered her mother, Amelia Dawley, teaching her the song as a child, led the family delegation in February 1997 to Sierra Leone, the country of her family's ancestry, as traced through the song. Amelia Dawley had learned the song from her grandmother. Mary Moran's son, Wilson, reminded symposium participants that language includes not only spoken words but also gestures and body language—including giving someone "de eye," as Gullah/Geechee elders are known to do to correct trouble-bound youths.

Translator Ardell Greene of Ridgeland, South Carolina, spoke about her initial reservations in 1979 concerning the Gullah Bible project. Following a trip to Jamaica in 1985, however, her sentiments changed. "My husband's wallet was coming out of his back pocket, and our taxi driver told him, `Mahn, you betta chook dat ting back een ya pocket for you ain hab no money fa git home!'

After that we said, `These people talk like us! It [Gullah] really is a language!'" Soon afterwards—at a Gullah festival in Beaufort, South Carolina—she witnessed a Jamaican woman pick up a copy of the 23rd Psalm in Gullah and read it without any trouble. "That made the Team members very excited!" she said.

Greene, a minister of the gospel, said the Gullah Bible has blessed her and will be a blessing to many. "When I prepare a sermon, first I read the King James version. Then I read the Gullah translation, and it really speaks to me. It speaks to me in my heart-tongue."

As translator Vernetta Canteen, also of Ridgeland, read John 1:1-18, the audience affirmed her Gullah presentation with sighs, gasps, chuckles, and, finally, applause.

> Fo God mek de wol, de Wod been dey. De Wod been dey wid God, an de Wod been God. Fo God mek de wol, de Wod been dey wid God. Shru dat Wod, God mek ebryting. Ain nottin een de whole wol wa God mek dat been done dout de Wod. De Wod, e de one wa all life come fom. An dis life yah de life wa da mek all people see de light. De light da shine een de daak, an de daak ain neba been able fa pit out dat light." (*De Nyew Testament*)

Their response validated that, for many, Gullah is the language they cry in, the language of their heart!

As emcee for the Gullah festival's opening ceremony on November 10, I read Luke 1:78–79 from *De Nyew Testament* and encouraged participants to let the light of God shine on them in order to guide their feet into the way of peace.

> Cause we God feel wa we feel, an e mussyful an do we good. E gwine mek de light ob sabation fa shine pon we like de sun ob day clean broad. Dat light gwine shine pon all de people wa lib een de daak shada ob det. E gwine hep we waak een a peaceable way.

Such is the goal of the Gullah Bible.

JAARS logo used for the release of the Gullah Bible.
Courtesy, JAARS, Inc.

E'r I get to the mountain top,
I praise my God and neva stop.

Photographer Leigh Richmond Miner's masterful pictorial documentations of Gullah lifestyles on St. Helena Island during the early 1900s grace my book *Reminiscences of Sea Island Heritage* as well as Edith M. Dabbs's *Face of an Island*. An educator at Hampton Institute and a native of Cornwall, Connecticut, Miner took photographs during his visits with former students who were teaching at the Penn Normal, Agricultural and Industrial School, which, in 1862, became the first school in the South for freed slaves.

Miner's personal mementos for the Daise family include a picture of my mother, Kathleen Grant Daise, at about nine years of age on the steps of the girls' dormitory at Penn School on Christmas morning, circa 1922 (Dabbs 1970). She and three other girls are clutching dolls that had been provided by the school's northern benefactors. Another prized photo (Daise 1986, 28), which predates my mother's birth in 1913, is of Ezekiel Grant, my grandfather, who died before his daughter was born. When I selected photographs for the book, I was unaware that the small-framed teacher, standing before barefoot and barely-shoed children at a one-room schoolhouse, was my grandfather! A Penn Center Museum docent identified him while she was culling through stacks of unidentified photos and artifacts years after the book's publication.

Miner's photographs show the lifestyles of my childhood, of living in an isolated Gullah community. Scenes of people making fish nets, toting objects on their heads, using mortars and pestles and grinding stones, and fishing from bateaus mirrored ones I grew up observing and had stored away in the recesses of my mind—then viewed in Ghana and Sierra Leone during 2004 and 2005.

During the period in which Miner was busy documenting my homeland on glass negatives, following the current technology, a Sierra Leonean musicologist was visiting St. Helena Island and conducting field research of spirituals as sung by Penn School students, community members, and vocal groups. I had been ignorant of Nicholas George Julius Ballanta's extensive work in ethnomusicology until my serendipitous visit in June 2005 during my participation in "Priscilla's Homecoming" to The Ballanta Academy of Music in Freetown, Sierra Leone, which he founded.

Ballanta, researching to find out what makes African music different from European music, had listened to the famed St. Helena Quartet, made up of individuals under whose guidance I grew up and who are pictured in *Reminiscences of Sea Island Heritage* (page 28). Aurelius "A. J." Brown, Benjamin "B. H." Washington, James "J. P." King, and Melvin T. Wildy were Penn School instructors who toured the United States performing Negro spirituals to raise funds for Penn School. Ballanta reveled in St. Helenians singing of the same spirituals I grew up hearing during worship services at Brick Baptist Church and leading at Community Sings at Penn Center, held the third Sunday evening of each month.

The air felt rarefied, charged with a sense of magic, as I walked through The Ballanta Academy and listened to African students sing Negro spirituals. Ballanta and I had walked on the same South Carolina soil.

The portrait of an elder Ballanta, which hangs in an academy classroom, resembled portraits of formerly enslaved African men Miner had captured on film during his forays to St. Helena. I felt a sense of wonder and amazement! Following my performance of "Something So Real!"—a song I had composed about Priscilla—at the U.S. Embassy, the academy's director urged me to visit before my departure from Sierra Leone. My doing so was a *must*, she implored.

I was happy to be able to fit a visit to the school into the exhaustive weeklong itinerary of activities. Before my trip to Ballanta Academy, "Priscilla's Homecoming" coordinator Joseph Opala informed me that Ballanta was to Negro spirituals what African-American linguist Lorenzo Dow Turner was to the Gullah language! Still, I was unprepared for what turned out to be a most captivating cultural encounter.

When I arrived, the twenty-something-member choir was rehearsing for an upcoming performance. The classroom, with its hardwood floors and folding wooden chairs, reminded me the Penn Center Library at Frissell Hall—a site of my childhood learning—and of events where sea island singers set a mesmerizing rhythm to shouting and somber spirituals by pounding their heels and clapping their hands to a distinguishable Gullah beat.

The singers, whose facial features and body movements mirrored those of people from my homeland, were enthralled to learn that I was from a community where their founder had conducted research during the early 1900s. The choir director could have passed for the twin of one of my fourth cousins. Marveling that I, like Ballanta, shared the importance of spirituals with others through my writings and performances, I told them about *Reminiscences of Sea Island Heritage* that included photographs of people whom Ballanta may very well have recorded during his field study. I sang for them spirituals from my book, which I like to imagine Ballanta heard during his visit.

Day is done.
Day is done.
Day is done.
I thank God day is done.

I work hard in the fields all day.
    I thank God day is done.
But I'm never too tired to pray.
    I thank God day is done.

Day is done.
Day is done.
Day is done.
I thank God day is done.

E'r I get to the mountain top—
    I thank God day is done.
I praise my God and never stop.
    I thank God day is done.

Day is done.
Day is done.
Day is done.
I thank God day is done. (44)

The choir members responded to my call. Their harmonies layered my lead. As voices and spirits connected, we knew that Ballanta would have been pleased.

Born March 14, 1893, in the village of Kissy in Freetown, Nicholas George Julius Ballanta became a composer, conductor, performer, and pioneering explorer of African indigenous music. Eldred D. Jones spoke eloquently of the musician's determination and accomplishments at the launching of the Ballanta Academy of Music on October 26, 1995:

> From his conventional beginnings he advanced to visions far beyond those of anyone else in his time and was, therefore, in some sense a lonely man. A visionary who cannot share his vision with his fellows is indeed a lonely man.
> Ballanta's researches into the aesthetics and philosophy of African music took him from Kissy to the Gambia to the United States to Germany and, above all, to many parts of Africa where he collected examples of African musical forms. (Wright, 2–3)

A graduate of Kissy Mission and Cathedral primary schools and the Christian Missionary Society Grammar School, Ballanta taught himself basic music theory and studied harmony and counterpoint through available text books. Recognizing a peculiar tone as he listened to a Bambara flautist and to Mendi folksongs "led him to conclude that African music must be different from European music and therefore must be governed by a different set of laws and principles which he felt he had to unravel." (Wright 5-8)

After a few fruitless years of collecting African folksongs and analyzing them according to western principles, Ballanta concluded that his objective could best be reached by traveling to the United States and studying Negro spirituals. He arrived in July 1921 and was disappointed to learn that no scientific research had been conducted about spirituals. He wrote, "Musicians in that country were then wondering what really was the origin of the Negro spiritual; they were asking themselves the question how it should be harmonised [sic]; and that tone which gave me trouble in the Gambia was very much in evidence as being one of the most disturbing facts which needed correlation. . . . It made itself felt in its passive state, occurring as it did in minor melodies as a raised sixth but without the usual procedure always allowed to such a tone in the minor scale. At the Gambia, it was given by an instrument; but in America, by the human voice; this shows that it is part of a perception, and makes it a point of much importance." (Wright, 10)

Philanthropist George Foster Peabody became a supporter of Ballanta's research at a time when the musicologist believed his project was doomed and planned to return to Sierra Leone. Peabody enabled Ballanta to study composition in the United States for an additional two years, during which time he executed his field work at Penn School on St. Helena Island. In the introduction to Ballanta's published collection of Negro spirituals at Penn School in 1922, Peabody wrote,

> He [Ballanta] . . . secured a first-hand knowledge of the music apparently so natural to the Negro population of the Southern states.
>
> While at Penn School this young man showed a peculiar facility in quickly and accurately recording the Spirituals as he heard them sung by the pupils, the Community Class connected with the school, and the St. Helena Quartet, which had done much to preserve the remarkably beautiful Spirituals of the Island. He was therefore requested to return and make a longer stay at Penn School for the purpose of recovering, if possible, as many as might be of these expressions of the great art instinct of the Negroes, as sung by old and young on St. Helena and nearby islands.
>
> This publication is the result of these thorough studies by Mr. Ballanta, who secured 103 Spirituals in versions not hitherto published, as it is believed. (Wright, 12–13)

From 1924 to early 1926, Ballanta toured Gambia, Sierra Leone, the Gold Coast, Nigeria, French and Portuguese Guinea, and Liberia. Afterward, at Berlin University, he studied the scientific relations of tones for about a year and a half. He, subsequently, produced two volumes in which he explained the principles of West African music: *The Aesthetics of African Music* and *The Philosophy of African Music.* He concluded that "the interesting thing about the African is that whilst he can naturally divide his notes into threes and sub-divisions of three, he is also capable of perceiving the duple sub-divisions at the same times as the triple sub-divisions. As a result, both elements may be combined, the time value of the pulse note being the same in both cases. When such combinations occur, there results that complexity in African rhythm which is acknowledged by anyone who is exposed to African drum music." (Wright, 20)

In 2004, sixth months after my return to South Carolina, I discovered a frayed pamphlet stored in a zip-locked plastic bag at a used and rare bookstore in downtown Beaufort. Too expensive to purchase, the yellowed paperback, *Saint Helena Island Spirituals (Recorded and Transcribed at Penn Normal, Industrial and Agricultural School)* by Nicholas George Julius Ballanta (© 1923), felt like gold leaf as I pored through its pages and identified twenty-seven spirituals with which I was familiar. These included "Sweet watah rollin'," "Come, come, come an go wid me," and "I'm a runnin' fo' muh life." I imagined Ballanta's pleasure at hearing them, and I remembered occasions when I had sung them.

The Ballanta Academy of Music was constructed in 1995, thirty-four years following Ballanta's death in 1961. Groups that study there include The Music Makers, Five Staves Brass, Young Ballanta Singers, African Drum Ensemble, Ballanta Baba Shop, and Jazz. (The Ballanta Academy of Music "Omnibus Ars Musica" brochure)

"Oh, let me shine, shine, shine like de mornin' star" was one of the 103 spirituals Ballanta recorded during field studies on St. Helena Island. My visit to the academy assured me that, throughout his life, he had done just that!

Learning about Ballanta's musical legacy inspired me to write a song about this cultural giant, utilizing the tune of "Day Is Done," a Gullah spiritual.

Nicholas George Julius Ballanta, an ethnomusicologist from Sierra Leone, conducted a field study of Negro spirituals on St. Helena Island during the early 1900s. Ballanta is to Negro spirituals what African American linguist Lorenzo Dow Turner is to Gullah language. Courtesy, Ballanta Academy of Music, Sierra Leone, Africa.

"Ballanta"

(Sung to the tune of Gullah spiritual "Day Is Done")

Ballanta
Ballanta
Ballanta, e bring de spirituals ta West Africa

A Sierra Leonean laan bout de Gullah song dem
       E bring de spirituals to West Africa
E gone Sout Calina fa yeddy dey song dem
       E bring de spirituals ta West Africa

Ballanta
Ballanta
Ballanta, e bring de spirituals ta West Africa

Dem song wa freemen sing on St. Helena Islan
       E bring de spirituals ta West Africa
Him write em een de fus spiritual publication
       E bring de spirituals ta West Africa

Ballanta
Ballanta
Ballanta, e bring de spirituals ta West Africa

Sence de early 1900s him de one show de connection
       E bring de spirituals ta West Africa
Wit West African an Gullah harmonies an rhydms
       E bring de spirituals ta West Africa

Ballanta
Ballanta
Ballanta, e bring de spirituals ta West Africa

Words by Ronald Daise
© 2005

"Hush, Somebody Callin My Name"

(Gullah spiritual)

Hush, hush, somebody callin my name
Hush, hush, somebody callin my name
Hush, hush, somebody callin my name
Oh, my Lawd; oh, my Lawd, what shall I do
What shall I do

Soon one mornin, Death come creepin een ma room
Soon one mornin, Death come creepin een ma room
Soon one mornin, Death come creepin een ma room
Oh, my Lawd; oh, my Lawd, what shall I do
What shall I do

Hush, hush, somebody callin my name
Hush, hush, somebody callin my name
Hush, hush, somebody callin my name
Oh, my Lawd; oh, my Lawd, what shall I do
What shall I do

Soun like Jesus, somebody callin my name
Soun like Jesus, somebody callin my name
Soun like Jesus, somebody callin my name
Oh, my Lawd; oh, my Lawd, what shall I do
What shall I do

Hush, hush, somebody callin my name
Hush, hush, somebody callin my name
Hush, hush, somebody callin my name
Oh, my Lawd; oh, my Lawd, what shall I do
What shall I do

I've been to Ghana and Sierra Leone.
I walked down the streets and felt right at home.
There's a connection deep down in my spirit
With Africa. West Africa.

"Symmetry, Balance, Peace"

The scenes I saw in Ghana and Sierra Leone—
like in other West African communities—
were like stepping back in time
on St. Helena Island
or Brookgreen, The Oaks, Laurel Hill, and Springfield Plantations
or Georgetown or Sandy Island
or numerous other communities along the Waccamaw Neck
or Charleston
or the Town of Mitchelville on Hilton Head Island
or Sapelo Island, Georgia—
in communities where Gullah and Geechee people have thrived.

Ghanaian girl balancing tray of fish on her head. Courtesy, Don Clerico, Professor of Education, Charleston Southern University, Charleston, South Carolina.

Woman at Ghanaian batik village using mortar and pestle (2004). Photo by author.

Fufu maker, using mortar and pestle. Courtesy, Don Clerico, Charleston Southern University.

In Ghana,
I saw palm trees with coconuts swaying in the breeze at Brenu Beach.
Slender wooden fishing boats rowed by slim, muscular men
from the nearby fisherman village
silhouetted the Atlantic.

Behind a restaurant,
as a backdrop on the horizon,
villagers passed
bearing bundles of sticks or logs on their heads
for firewood.

Others bent and toiled in their fields
or carted wheelbarrows.
Children rolled spokeless bike wheels
or played soccer—
dressed in brown and yellow uniforms—
at the nearby village schoolyard.
Goats ambled among the seated beachgoers
and among the Ghanaian villagers.
There was symmetry and balance. . . .
There was peace wafting on the cool breeze. . . .
The pastoral farmland was not a golf course.
The workers in the fields were not tourists at some chic mall.
The beach was open to all—not a private, gated recluse
for condominium owners only.
The waitress and the cook weren't eye candy.
They were living their daily lives
as they do from day to day
without distinction to whomever came to the beach.
Nearby, uniformed children played on a bamboo slide.

The scenes are reminders of proud,
self-sufficient,
self-possessed Gullah/Geechee landowners
whose lives sing *Walk Togedda, Chirren, Dontcha Git Weary*—
who know *Creata Gawd own de lan. De lan don own we!*
and who, therefore, believe
De lan, de wata, de eart blongst ta ebryboddy! Enty dat so?
who, nonetheless, hold onto their land for future generations
cause dis lan de lan wa great-great granddaddy buy longtime gone
an sacafice fa keep
mm-hmm, dis lan we ownt
an een dis lan we fin peace.

(Opposite, top) "Teaching & Learning in Ghana 2004" participants Beth Williams (Sprauve), Ron, and N'Kia Jones (Campbell) enjoy a visit to Brenu Beach.
Photos courtesy, Don Clerico, Charleston Southern University.

Photos courtesy,
Don Clerico, Charleston
Southern University.

In Sierra Leone, worshipers gathered
at Star of the Sea Catholic Church in Juba Village, Freetown,
to honor the homecoming
of Priscilla,
the ten-year-old Sierra Leonean girl
captured and enslaved in 1756
and taken to a rice plantation in South Carolina.
Her great-great-great-great-great granddaughter,
Thomalind Martin Polite,
of Charleston, South Carolina
with husband Antawn,
were being welcomed ceremoniously for returning Priscilla's spirit
home
nearly 250 years later.

Dancers in ceremonial tribal make-up worship in honor of Priscilla at Our Lady Star of the Sea Parish service in Juba Village, Freetown, Sierra Leone. Photo by author.

Dancers lead processional into sanctuary. Courtesy, Leslie Anderson Morales.

Members of the Catholic Women's Association gathered to pay homage to Priscilla and her 7th-generation descendant. Courtesy, Leslie Anderson Morales.

There was symmetry,
balance,
peace
as members of the Catholic Women's Association,
the C.W.A.,
uniformed in deep blue dresses—
"flee-from-me-hags and haints-blue" dresses
with matching headwraps—
assembled to pay homage
to the descendant of their sister who had left their country's shores
so long ago,
so very
long
ago.
The ceremony stirred within me
youthful reminiscences of
Gullah community Baptist church usher or choir anniversaries
with pomp and pageantry and power—
that "fill-this-temple-with-your-presence, Lord!" kind of power.
The processional commenced with praiseful dancing
of six young females dressed in white tops
and colorful blue print skirts.
Their faces, spirit-like and worshipful, were painted white with clay
in honor of elders, in homage to ancestors.
Robed bearers of incense followed.

Before instrumentalists entered,
the rhythms of drums and shakares and balanjis filled each corner of the sanctuary.
With African harmonies, jubilant and reverent,
choir members stepped in—
dressed in green robes with gold trimming and green caps with gold tassels.
Such symmetry.
Such balance.
Such peace.
Members of the C.W.A. processed like regal, spiritual warriors
preparing the way for Parish Priest,
the Reverend Father Ambrose M. Damba
—tall and regal, dark and bearing a mantle of divinity—

who upon entering
flailed holy water onto congregants
with a palm frond dipped frequently into a blue pail.

And in Dunkegba Village,
men and women pounded handmade mortars and pestles
that are used daily in their rice village.
Their demonstrations are to the rhythm,
the same rhythm,
that their Gullah descendants
pounded grains of rice
on South Carolina and Georgia plantations
some 200 years ago.

Sierra Leonean women demonstrate using a shukably fannem
basket and a mortar and pestle
for hulling rice during a celebration at Dunkegba Village.

Courtesy, Toni Carrrier, Joyce Reese
McCollum, and the Africana Heritage
Project, Tampa, Florida,
www.africanaheritage.com.

Before my eyes,
Present became Past.
Past became Present.

There was symmetry.
There was balance.
There was peace.

I'm gonna sing so God can use me any time, any time, any where.

"While your presence on the Homecoming would be a benefit to Sierra Leoneans who will learn more about Gullah culture through your performances," historian Joseph Opala stated in a letter of invitation for me to participate in Priscilla's Homecoming, "you will also have much to give people back here in the U.S. upon your return. Because you are an educator, you will be in a position for years to talk about the Homecoming, to show the documentary film, and to teach about the Gullah people's link to Sierra Leone."

One of the researchers who uncovered portions of the story linking Priscilla to Sierra Leone, Opala coordinated Priscilla's Homecoming along with Charleston filmmaker Jacque Metz. At the printing of this book, on-location filming of the event is in post-production for broadcast as a documentary on PBS or another educational channel and distribution to schools and colleges throughout the country.

Priscilla's Homecoming, a non-profit activity, was Opala's fourth coordination of a Gullah homecoming to Sierra Leone since 1988. The first began after former Sierra Leonean president Joseph Mohmoh learned from Opala about cultural ties of West African heritage among the Gullah people of South Carolina and Georgia. Mohmoh visited the South Carolina Lowcountry communities of Beaufort and St. Helena Island in 1988. During his visit, I was honored to recite the Gullah biblical story "De Exaddis"—about the deliverance of the Hebrew children—before His Excellency during a reception at a Beaufort hotel (Daise and Daise 1993). Afterward, Mohmoh proclaimed that the recitation sounded like that of a Liberian preacher—a speaker of Liberian English, a dialect similar to Gullah. At Penn Center on St. Helena Island, Mohmoh spoke before an expectant audience in Krio, which the Gullah residents understood. They conversed in Gullah, which he, likewise, understood.

The documentary film *Family Across the Sea* chronicled a contingent of

Gullah residents traveling to Sierra Leone at President Mohmoh's request in 1989. The Gullah homecoming was led by Emory Campbell, executive director of Penn Center. My wife Natalie and I were to have participated in this event, but the birth of our firstborn, Sara, prohibited our traveling.

The second homecoming in 1997, that of the Moran family, resulted in the documentary film *The Language You Cry In*. During research following the first homecoming, it was discovered that an elderly resident of Harris Neck, Georgia, remembered a song she'd been taught by her grandmother, who had been a slave. She didn't know anything about the song except the tune and the African words. Opala carried a recording of the song made by Lorenzo Turner in 1981 to numerous Sierra Leonean villages and discovered that the song is a funeral dirge, still remembered in one village in the Mende region.

Opala's invitation to me to join the 2005 excursion could not have come at a better time. I had recently begun working as Vice President for Creative Education at Brookgreen Gardens. My participation would enable me to augment my repository of information about Gullah history and culture and the significant skills and knowledge of the enslaved West African labor force, which sustained the rice economy throughout the slave era. During that period, tens of thousands of Africans from Senegal, Gambia, Sierra Leone, Ghana, Angola, and numerous other West and Central African countries were captured and brought to the rice, indigo, and cotton plantations of coastal South Carolina and Georgia. In the town of Georgetown, South Carolina, and neighboring island communities along the Waccamaw River, demographics from the 1700s through early 1900s indicate a population ratio of about 8,000 Africans to 100 whites. The Africans maintained the customs, beliefs, work ethic, art forms, and speech of their forebears because of the isolation of the plantation communities, which were connected by bridges beginning only in the mid-1900s.

A fourth-generation descendant of transplanted West Africans, I was born on St. Helena Island before Gullah heritage was esteemed or popularized. When I was growing up, no one wanted to be identified as a Geechee, and the word Gullah was rarely used. As a pattern of speech or a way of life, the use of either term was considered a mark of shame or embarrassment. The marshfront and ocean-view family plots of my childhood, which today are million-dollar real estate properties, were communities where goats, cows, and other farm animals ambled and sustenance farms etched the landscape. In these communities, men and women landowners walked with a gait of dignity and pride. And though they and their children spoke what was called "broken English," the heritage they passed on was complete because of respect for elders, spirituality and love of God, and the knowledge that "community" meant all who lived therein, whether or not related by blood.

In Ghana and in Sierra Leone, I had experiences similar to ones I recall from my early days at Hampton University in Hampton, Virginia. At Hampton I was three states away and several hundred miles from home, but that first day I heard a familiar form of speech at the table behind me in the cafeteria. I turned quickly and approached my new classmates who, I discovered, hailed from the Virgin Islands. We spoke "cousin" creole languages, with shared grammatical rules such as substituting "skr" for "str" at the beginning of words such as strong, making *skrong*; and substituting "d" or "t" for "th," as in *dis* for this and *ting* for thing. The creole patois of Gullah began as trade languages on African slave-holding stations and slave ships. The Africans, assembled from numerous tribes and countries and speaking numerous languages, created a common language in order to communicate. On the island plantations of South Carolina and Georgia, that trade language became the dominant language, which is still spoken today. Many words are English, but the syntax is largely West African. In fact, the *lingua franca* Krio spoken in Sierra Leone remarkably resembles Gullah.

While a student at Hampton University, I met West Africans, primarily from Nigeria, who looked like family members or resembled people from South Carolina sea island communities. They told me they had left someone who looked like me on a mountain or in a village in Africa, and we readily understood each other when we spoke. They also told me that I carried myself differently and had a different mindset than other African-American students on campus. This scenario played out again and again as I walked throughout Ghana with fellow American participants in the "Teaching and Learning in Ghana" program. Elder Ghanaians would approach me quietly when the white educators walked away and begin speaking in Fante, assured that I understood them. I was told later they assumed me to be Ghanaian or another African nationality—but not African-American. Although I learned a few words of Fante during my five-week stay, my response to them was to look them in the eyes, point to myself while shaking my head, and say, "American." They wanted to be understood, and I wanted to understand them. The English spoken by Ghanaians who were my contemporaries or younger rolled onto my ears as comfortably as conversations with Gullah speakers, but many of the Ghanaian elders spoke Fante only.

Krio, the *lingua franca* of Sierra Leone, was much easier to understand. Gullah and Krio share similar words and expressions, like the greeting "How oona do?" (Gullah) and "Au una du?" (Krio) for "How are you?" A Sierra Leonean also may ask in Krio, "Au di bohdy?"—for which the response would be "Di bohdy fain!" or "A tel Gohd tenki!"

When my son Simeon was born, my pet name for him became "Bobo." I had no idea where my mind came up with that! I was astounded to learn later, while in Sierra Leone, that "bohboh" is Krio for "boy." "Bobo" is also the Ghanaian name for a male born on Monday, as my son was.

One of my Gullah performances in Sierra Leone was at the official residence of U.S. Ambassador and Mrs. Thomas N. Hull. I presented the story "De Exaddis," which I had shared with President Mohmoh in 1988. This time, as on the previous trip, I received looks of astonishment and recognition from listeners. Sierra Leoneans understood Gullah.

*The Ambassador of the United States of America
& Mrs. Thomas N. Hull*

request the honor of the presence of

__Mr. Daise__

at a Reception

*In honor "Priscilla's Homecoming" to
Sierra Leone*

Sunday, May 29, 2005

5:30 – 7:00 P.M.

R.S.V.P.   *American Ambassador's Residence*
226-481 Ext 261   *Signal Hill Roundabout*
Dress: Smart Casual   *Please bring this card along*

Invitation to Priscilla's Homecoming reception at the American Ambassador's residence.

Priscilla's Homecoming participant Charles Black, Freetown Players director Charlie Haffner, Ron, and Freetown Players member Mohammed Gemmeh Kargbo reminisce about the evening's events at Ambassador Hull's reception. Courtesy, Charlie Haffner.

My presentation at Star of the Sea Catholic Church in Juba Village, Freetown, was unforgettable. I read the scripture John 6:51–58 in Gullah from *De Good Nyews Wa John Write*, which the Reverend Father Ambrose M. Damba had read earlier in English. As I read, gasps and shrieks and hushed-but-excited laughter began to ripple through the sanctuary. Words and expressions, such as "gii" for give, "dis" for this, "bex" for vexed or confused, and "nyam" for eat, were readily understood by the church members.

Throughout "Priscilla's Homecoming," as I recited Krio words with their Gullah complements, I'd remember the tune of a Gullah children's song and begin humming. I'd heard "Ol Lady Come from Boosta" sung onstage by the legendary Miss Janie Hunter of Johns Island, South Carolina, during the late 1980s. More recently, others may have heard the song sung by my high school classmate and friend Anita Singleton Prather (also known as "Aunt Pearlie Sue"), who has resurrected many songs from Miss Hunter's repertoire.

> Ol Lady come from Boosta
> She had ten hen an a roosta
> De roosta die; de ol lady cry
> She couldn git aig like she useta.

I used the tune to create a song called "Gullah Cousin ta Krio." An A tell Gawd "tenki" ebryboddy wa yeddy em now kin know dat, fa true!

"Gullah Cousin ta Krio"

(Sung to the tune of Gullah children's song "Ol Lady Come from Boosta")

CHORUS:
Gullah cousin ta Krio.
Same taak, same soun. Yeah, dat so!
When A say a wod. Repeat wa you heard.
Dey cousin-tongue, fa true. You see-oh.

Een Gullah we say "dis"; een Krio dey say "dis" (for *this*)
Een Gullah we say "dat"; een Krio dey say "dat" (for *that*)
Een Gullah we say "oona"; een Krio dey say "una" (for *you*)
Een Gullah we say "ooman"; een Krio dey say "uman" (for *woman*)

REFRAIN:
Yeah, we taak de same way—small small, small small
Yeah, we taak de same way—small small, small small

CHORUS

Een Gullah we say "haid"; een Krio dey say "eyd" (for *head*)
Een Gullah we say "mout"; een Krio dey say "moht" (for *mouth*)
Een Gullah we say "yez"; een Krio dey say "yeys" (for *ears*)
Een Gullah we say "yeddy"; een Krio dey say "yeri" (for *hear*)

REFRAIN

CHORUS

Een Gullah we say "whodat?"; een Krio dey say "udat?" (for *who?*)
Een Gullah we say "big eye"; een Krio dey say "big yai" (for *greedy*)
Een Gullah we say "glad tummoch"; een Krio dey say "gladi tumohs" (for *happy*)
Een Gullah we say "tank ya now"; een Krio dey say "tenki" (for *thank you*)

Now fa plurals we bot do de same ting—we add eida "dem" or "den"

chirren dem	pikin den
shoes dem	sus den
hand dem	an den

Clap yo hand dem, sing wit me now

CHORUS:
Gullah cousin ta Krio.
Same taak, same soun. Yeah, dat so!
Some wod dem dey de same.
Now yeddy me plain:
Dey cousin-tongue, fa true. You see-oh.

Words by Ronald Daise
© 2005

I know de Lawd, I know de Lawd,
I know de Lawd has laid His hands on me.

For years, Gullah people found it shameful and embarrassing to be identified as such—in part because we thought our heritage began as slaves. We've heard the terms "Gullah" and "Geechee" spewed as invectives to discredit and humiliate, and only within the recent past has information been documented and accepted that invalidates this assertion. In fact, the term "African slaves" spawned ire during discussions at a 2005 board meeting for the developing International African American Museum in Charleston, of which I am a member.

"Africans were *not* slaves!" fellow board member James E. Campbell argued vehemently. "They were *not* slaves when they lived in Africa, and they were *not* slaves when they were brought into the port at Sullivans Island. Slavery was an act of conditioning, and many Africans resisted it. They were *enslaved*. They were *not* slaves."

Afterward, Campbell, a retired educator who was born in and now resides in Charleston, explained, "African people were taken out of Africa. They were forced into migration through the MIDDLE PASSAGE voyage and then enslaved in what was then Colonial America, the Caribbean and South America, among other places. In the case of the American enslavement of African people, this would continue on, into and under the new Federal Constitution, only reaching a partial resolution in the southern suicide of Civil War.

"African people were off-loaded at Sullivan's Island. At that juncture, they were captured Africans. ENSLAVEMENT was a process of organized, systematic and pervasive violence waged against these African people whose labor power was central to the building of South Carolina and the emerging United States of America. Enslaved African Labor was central to the development of Capitalism on a global scale. South Carolina was an integral part and player in that global economic process based on enslaved African labor energy—unpaid!

"People—African People—were forcibly taken out of Africa and enslaved.

This is key to asserting and reaffirming the basic humanity of our early ancestors in this strange land."

Cynthia H. Porcher, principal researcher for the five-year study of Gullah culture for the National Park Service, said she faced challenges of having persons talk about uncomfortable topics such as slavery.

"I learned a great deal about how unhappy slaves were and how there were work stoppages and slow-downs and sickouts and all kinds of things on the plantations," she stated in a newspaper interview. "They were not happy-clappy black faces and mammies with big smiles. There may have been people like that, who were very close to the families who owned them, but for the most part, that was a myth. And there is not enough emphasis on how much of a myth that is." ("Gullah culture study complete," *The Beaufort Gazette*, December 27, 2005, 3A)

Gullah ancestry includes not only a history of having endured slavery but also of possessing the skills and knowledge about rice production that provided the backbone of South Carolina's and Georgia's rice economy in the 1800s. Rice production, in fact, was an integral part of their West African cultural identity. For that reason, the skills of these individuals were highly esteemed by plantation owners in the New World. The forebears of these enslaved Africans came from cultures where rice production continues to this day.

Africans from countries of the Rice Coast (Senegal, Gambia, Guinea-Bissau, Guinea, Sierra Leone, and Liberia) knew firsthand how to clear swamps, use tides to irrigate fields, build dikes for flooding and clearing the fields, and coat the rice seeds when planting so they wouldn't float to the surface. Enslaved women aboard the slave ships knew how to process the rice that had been stored aboard for fattening the Africans following the arduous twelve-week journey to the New World, known as the Middle Passage ("Low Country Gullah Culture Special Resource Study," 25).

In "The Introduction of Black Slavery in Georgia" (1974) Betty C. Wood wrote:

> When New World slaves planted rice in the spring by pressing a hole with the heel and covering the seeds with the foot, the motion used was demonstrably similar to that employed in West Africa. In summer, when Carolina blacks moved through the rice fields in a row, hoeing in unison to work songs, the pattern of

cultivation was not imposed by European owners but rather one retained from West African forebears. And in October when the threshed grain was "fanned" in the wind, the wide, flat winnowing baskets were made by black hands after an African design.

Rice exports from South Carolina began at about 12,000 pounds in 1698 and rose to 18 million pounds in 1730. In 1770, 83 million pounds were exported, predominately from South Carolina and Georgia ("Low Country Gullah Culture Special Resource Study," 26). In Georgetown County, South Carolina, alone during the 1850s, 45,000 acres of rice fields spanned the landscape.

"We must look at history with new eyes," said Michael Allen, National Park Service ranger on Sullivan's Island and researcher for the "Low Country Gullah Special Resource Study." "This requires us to take a hard look at the past to understand the present and to prepare for the future. I believe that on many occasions African Americans are unwilling to look at history because of the impact slavery has made in the black community. Often such attitudes can serve as a form of bondage when you are living in the 21st century but trying to practice 18th-century customs.

"Over the course of the past six years I have been blessed to travel from one end to the other end of the Gullah Geechee Coast. My experiences have provided me with a wonderful opportunity to view Gullah history in a whole different light. When folks take the opportunity to learn and experience Gullah Geechee culture and to get to know folks, one cannot help but to view history with new eyes.

"Unfortunately, African American history in the state of South Carolina has often been neglected, ignored and pushed aside. Therefore, in my work I had to be very careful that I did not develop similar attitudes about Gullah Geechee Culture. I would hope that the Gullah Geechee Project would serve as a vehicle for change by offering the citizens of this state and the nation an opportunity to view history with new eyes.

"Secondly, I would hope that the eyes of government officials might be open and that a change of attitude would occur in how the affairs of this state are handled in context of African American history. Perhaps this new vision will allow officials to see Coastal development with a new set of eyes. Hopefully, these new eyes will be used to see the past and to help folks to stop overlooking Gullah Culture in efforts to develop the Landscape. `New Eyes' means that elected officials will take the time to visit Gullah communities, ask questions, and seek solutions to the age-old question regarding the importance of Gullah Culture. I would encourage everyone to view history with new eyes in an effort to bring about improved understanding of Local, State, National and International History. Truly, when all of this is in place, all will be looking at history with a new set of eyes."

With a new set of eyes, as Allen maintains, Gullah and Geechee people will realize that their West African ancestors had not been slaves—that they came from cultures where rice production continues to this day. As is expressed in the words of the re-lyriced spiritual "Well Known fa Growin Rice," being called a "Rice-Eating Geechee" or a "Fresh-Water Gullah"—instead of bringing embarrassment—should bring about a sense of pride!

"Well Known fa Growin Rice"

(Sung to the tune of Gullah spiritual "Soon A Will Be Done")

CHORUS:
Sierra Leoneans were well known fa growin rice
Well known fa growin rice, well known fa growin rice
Slave traders sought them out and for them paid a higha price
They were skilled
They were not born slaves

CHORUS:
Sierra Leoneans were well known fa growin rice
Well known fa growin rice, well known fa growin rice
Slave traders sought them out and for them paid a higha price
They were skilled
They were not born slaves

Fa centries, dey had labored een de rice fields
Wit handmade tools dey worked een de rice fields
Plantin, harvestin, poundin een de rice fields
They were skilled they were not born slaves

Dere country's bout de size ob Sout Calina
De climate's bout de same as een Sout Calina
De lan look like home when een Sout Calina
They were skilled
They were not born slaves

CHORUS:
Sierra Leoneans were well known fa growin rice
Well known fa growin rice, well known fa growin rice
Slave traders sought them out and for them paid a higha price
They were skilled
They were not born slaves

De plantas didn know rice production
Dey needed workas who knew rice production
Sierra Leoneans knew rice production
They were skilled
They were not born slaves

De plantas grew rich from de slave trade
Bot homes, oh, were destroyed by de slave trade
De African fambly was uprooted by de slave trade
They were skilled
They were not born slaves

CHORUS:
Sierra Leoneans were well known fa growin rice
Well known fa growin rice, well known fa growin rice
Slave traders sought them out and for them paid a higha price
They were skilled
They were not born slaves
They were skilled
They were not born slaves
They were skilled
They were not born slaves

Words by Ronald Daise
© 2005

Milk an honey oba dere een me Fadah house.

Just as milk and honey are the anticipated nectar of those who cross over to heaven, as proclaimed in many spirituals, rice and rice dishes are necessary dietary staples of daily (or regular) consumption for Gullahs and Geechees.

The tens of thousands of visitors who participate in the Penn Center Heritage Days Festival (second weekend of November, St. Helena Island, South Carolina), the Gullah Festival (Memorial Day weekend, Beaufort, South Carolina), the Hilton Head Island (South Carolina) Gullah Celebration (each weekend in February), and the Georgia Sea Island Festival (fall, St. Simon's Island) feast on numerous rice dishes in honor of Gullah heritage. These include red rice, also known as mulatto rice; rice pilau (or perlow)—rice-n-oysters, rice-n-shrimp, rice-n-collards, beans-n-rice, or sweet peas-n-rice; pork chops-n-gravy ova rice; gumbo ova rice; oxtail, stringbeans, and potatoes ova rice; conch soup-n-rice; stewed fish or chicken ova rice; eggs-n-rice; and hoppin' john (or field peas-n-rice).

West African cuisine offers similar rice dishes, as I've sampled in Ghana and Sierra Leone. In Krio, A tel Gohd tenki wey res bin dey plenti wey a bin dey na Salon. The foods helped me feel at home during my visits. In like manner, pots full of rice, I'm certain, helped Gullah forebears on South Carolina and Georgia plantations quell pangs of homesickness after being uprooted from West African shores.

Rice has been, is, and ever shall be important to people of West African heritage! During the 1800s at Brookgreen Plantation, an average weekly food ration included ten quarts of rice or peas. Goliath, a former slave of F. W. Allston, owner of Brookgreen, ca. 1937, used the following indigenous and essential recipe:

> Fust t'ing yo' roll up yo' sleeve 'es high as yo' kin, en yo' tak soap en yo' wash yo' hand clean. Den yo' wash yo' pot clean.

Fill um wid col' wata en put on de fia. Now w'ile you' wata bile, yo' put yo' rice een a piggen en yo' wash um well. Den when yo' dun put salt een yo' pot, en bile high. Yo' put yo rice een en le-um bile til 'e swell, den yo' pour off de wata en put yo' pot back o de stove, fo' steam. ("Low Country Gullah Special Resource Study," 55)

The documentary *The Language You Cry In* (1998) details a Sierra Leonean burial custom in which rice was used. For the Mende graveside Tenjami ceremony, villagers cooked rice and blended it with meat from a sacrificed animal, palm oil, and salt. This was then dished onto a banana leaf and placed on the grave while villagers sang,

A wa kaka, mu mohne; kambei ya le'i; lii i lei tambee
A wa kaka, mu mohne; kambei ya le'i; lii i lei kaka (Opala 1988, 34)

At the conclusion of the ceremony, the empty large cast iron pot was turned upside down on top of the grave, and the village children feasted on the leftover rice.

The Mende words of "Amelia Dawley's Song" linked the family of Amelia Dawley of Harris Neck, Georgia, to their Sierra Leonean ancestors. Dawley, who had learned the song from her grandmother and taught it to her own daughter, recorded it as an adult for African-American linguist Lorenzo Dow Turner during the early 1930s. It was included in Turner's groundbreaking field study, which used African songs and story texts, documenting Gullah as a language. What served as a funeral song in Africa had become a play song in America, sung to children by their mothers.

During the 1980s, Joseph Opala began researching the origin of the five-line song heard in Turner's recording. The song, believed to have been brought by an enslaved African woman during the 1700s to a Georgia rice plantation near Harris Neck, eventually connected her family to the rice culture of Sierra Leone.

As translated by Tazieff Koroma, Edward Benya, and Joseph Opala, the song's lyrics cry out:

Everyone come together, let us work hard;

The grave is not yet finished; let his heart be perfectly at peace.

Everyone come together, let us work hard:

The grave is not yet finished; let his heart be at peace at once. ("Low Country Gullah Culture Special Resource Study," 60)

"With rice they bid farewell to those who leave this world and welcome them to the realm of the ancestors," Vertamae Grosvenor narrates in *The Language You Cry In*. And in some West African cultures, even today, as Joseph Opala lectured during a "Priscilla's Homecoming" presentation, "Rice flour is a sacred item."

Today, in Gullah communities, rice dishes please the eyes and palettes at family reunions, church anniversaries, weddings, and funeral repasts. Gullahs, Sierra Leoneans, West Africans, and others of the African Diaspora sometimes joyfully consume rice three times daily. "No, we cyahn go an not eat rice or we belly fa rice will pray!"

"De Rice Sing"

(Chorus is sung to the tune of Sierra Leonean folk song "Home Again")

CHORUS:
Een Salone dey eat rice, fa true
An de Gullahs eat rice—dat so
Sometime shree time a day
No, we cyahn go and not eat rice
Or we belly fa rice will pray

CHORUS:
Een Salone dey eat rice, fa true
An de Gullahs eat rice—dat so
Sometime shree time a day
No, we cyahn go and not eat rice
Or we belly fa rice will pray

Anh-hanh. A break eet dong.

RAP #1
Now dere's de Jollof Rice
Wit tomatas, onions, beef, n peppa seasonins, too
De Gullahs call dat dish Red or Mulatto Rice.
E mek de belly feel good. Fa true!

RAP #2
Now ova de rice pit cassava leaves
Mix wit fish n beef n beans.
Dat like de Gullah dish, Collard greens n rice
Cook wit fatback—e tase supreme!

Pat yo belly. Pat yo belly.

CHORUS:
Een Salone dey eat rice, fa true
An de Gullahs eat rice—dat so
Sometime shree time a day
No, we cyahn go and not eat rice
Or we belly fa rice will pray

A break eet dong fa oona—one time gen.

RAP #3
New Year's Eve, Gullahs eat Hoppin John fa luck—
Dats field peas cook wit rice.
Een Salone, dey eat Abobo—black-eyed peas
Mix wit plantains—Mek de rice mo nice!

RAP # 4
Now dere's de Peppa Chicken n de Groundnut Stew
Dere's de rice n okra, too.
We eyes open wide when dey see rice fa eat
An we belly tell we teet, "Time fa chew!"

Pat yo belly. Crack ya teet!

CHORUS:
Een Salone dey eat rice, fa true
An de Gullahs eat rice—dat so
Sometime shree time a day
No, we cyahn go and not eat rice
Or we belly fa rice will pray

Words by Ronald Daise
© 2005
(NOTE: In old Gullah speech, the word
"sing" was used for the word "song.")

Menu at the Sierra Leonean buffet lunch, Cape Lighthouse Hotel, Aberdeen.

<u>**MENU**</u>

Jollof Rice & Stew – Rice, Tomatoes, Onions, Garden eggs, Pepper, oil, Beef, seasonings

Groundnut Soup & Funde – Groundnuts, onions tomatoes, peppers, okra, fish, beef, funde (millet)

Cassava Leaves & Rice – Cassava Leaves, Beans sesame paste, palmoil , dried fish, Beef

Foofoo & White Sawa – Cassava, Egusi (Melon seeds) Sesame Paste, Beef Tripe, Sawa sawa leaves, Dried fish

Palm Oil Stew & Country Rice – fresh fish, onions, pepper, tomatoes, spring onions, seasoning

Abobo (Black eye beans, Plantain & Sweet Potatoe), **Rice Akara, Beans Akara**

Pepper Chicken –Chicken, Groundnut paste lime & seasonings

Roast Meat – Beef, groundnut, lime, & seasonings

Salad – Lettuce, tomatoes, cucumbers,spring onions

Fruit Salad – Mango, pineapple, banana, oranges, grape fruit

Rice Bead, coconut cake, groundnut cake

Ginger beer, Tombi drink, Palm wine

"I'm Gonna Sing So God Can Use Me"

(Gullah spiritual)

I'm gonna sing so God can use me anytime, anytime, anywhere
I'm gonna sing so God can use me anytime, anytime, anywhere

I'm gonna pray so God can use me anytime, anytime, anywhere
I'm gonna pray so God can use me anytime, anytime, anywhere

I'm gonna live so God can use me anytime, anytime, anywhere
I'm gonna live so God can use me anytime, anytime, anywhere

I'm gonna love so God can use me anytime, anytime, anywhere
I'm gonna love so God can use me anytime, anytime, anywhere

"In My Father's House"

(Gullah spiritual)

Come and go with me to my Father's house, to my Father's house,
    to my Father's house
Come and go with me to my Father's house
There is joy, joy, joy

No more crying over there in my Father's house, in my Father's
    house, in my Father's house
No more crying over there in my Father's house
There is joy, joy, joy

No more sorrow over there in my Father's house, in my Father's
    house, in my Father's house
No more sorrow over there in my Father's house
There is joy, joy, joy

Milk and honey over there in my Father's house, in my Father's
    house, in my Father's house
Milk and honey over there in my Father's house
There is joy, joy, joy

"I Know the Lord Has Laid His Hands on Me"

(Gullah spiritual)

I know the Lord, I know the Lord, I know the Lord has laid His
    hands on me.
I know the Lord, I know the Lord, I know the Lord has laid His
    hands on me.

I never been to heaven, but I been tol
        I know the Lord has laid His hands on me
The streets up there are paved with gold
        I know the Lord has laid His hands on me

I know the Lord, I know the Lord, I know the Lord has laid His
    hands on me.
I know the Lord, I know the Lord, I know the Lord has laid His
    hands on me.

If you get there before I do
        I know the Lord has laid His hands on me
Tell all my friends I'm comin home, too
        I know the Lord has laid His hands on me

I know the Lord, I know the Lord, I know the Lord has laid His
    hands on me.
I know the Lord, I know the Lord, I know the Lord has laid His
    hands on me.

"Soon A Will Be Done wit de Trouble of de Worl"

(Gullah spiritual)

Soon A will be done wit de trouble of de worl
De trouble of de worl, de trouble of de worl
Soon A will be done wit de trouble of de worl
Goin home ta lib wit God

A wan ta see my modda
A wan ta see my modda
A wan ta see my modda
Goin home ta lib wit God

Soon A will be done wit de trouble of de worl,
De trouble of de worl, de trouble of de worl
Soon A will be done wit de trouble of de worl
Goin home ta lib wit God

No mo weepin an a-wailin
No mo weepin an a-wailin
No mo, no mo weepin an a-wailin
Goin ta lib wit God

Soon A will be done wit de trouble of de worl,
De trouble of de worl, de trouble of de worl
Soon A will be done wit de trouble of de worl
Goin home ta lib wit God

I looked into dark faces everywhere I'd go.
Something behind their eyes let me know
There's a connection deep down in my spirit
With Africa. West Africa.

"Free!"

Ghana, West Africa,
whose citizens tout it as "The Friendliest Country in Africa"
and "The Gateway to Africa"
is a place where everyone can feel
FREE!
Free, yes, just as one feels in Gullah communities . . .
Rich or poor,
African or European,
White or African-American,
Protestant or Moslem
Catholic or Yoruba
illiterate or educated,
political or non-conformist,
pedestrian or cyclist or chauffeured,
naked or regally dressed,
everyone,
when in Ghana,
can drop their masks
their camouflages,
their barriers
that prohibit them from connecting with others
and even with themselves
and
just
be
FREE!

Courtesy, Don Clerico,
Charleston Southern University.

59

Photos courtesy, Don Clerico, Charleston Southern University.

You feel this as you walk through the marketplaces
and visit government offices and cultural institutions.
As you listen to the music
and look into the eyes of the elderly.
As you worship in churches or mosques
and watch native artisans carve wood, batik fabric, weave kente cloth, thread jewelry.
Freedom and dignity
mark
the faces of the miners of gold,
the speech of the tour guides who tell about Ghana's history,
culture
and political struggles.

Photo by author.

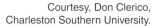

Courtesy, Don Clerico,
Charleston Southern University.

Photos courtesy, Don Clerico,
Charleston Southern University.

Photos courtesy, Don Clerico, Charleston Southern University.

Freedom and dignity
mark
the smile of the children,
yes, the children,
who are the hope of any country.
Just as one feels in Gullah communities,
when in Ghana
one can feel
FREE!

Courtesy, Don Clerico, Charleston Southern University.

He didn't have to do it, but He did.

My first glance into the face of fourteen-year-old Carlos Muta brought little recognition. It was evening, and the eleven other teachers and I were tired after a long bus ride from Cape Coast to Tamale along bladder-jarring African dirt roads. Following dinner, I noticed Carlos speaking quietly with some of the female African-American participants in the "Teaching and Learning in Ghana 2004" (TLG) program. I caught his eyes only cursorily, thinking he—like numerous other Ghanaian children who had hovered near our bus when we arrived in different towns—was hawking wares and trinkets.

As we readied to depart the hotel the next morning, Carlos hovered again. This time we spoke.

"I want to go to school," he pleaded. "Can you help me to go to school?" I searched his eyes to discern honesty before dispersing cedis, Ghanaian currency, and asking appropriate questions. In a flash of African sunlight, I recognized a familiar skin tone and facial bone structure, a slanting of the forehead, a bulging of the nose bridge. I stared more intently, my eyes widening, and then alerted one of my TLG mates.

"Who does he look like?" I asked.

"Um, huh, like you, Ron!" was the response. Others began to point and comment, and our bus driver and guide called for us to board.

I learned that Carlos, the eldest of five children, was from Yon Village, about five hours away. His nineteen-year-old uncle had brought him to Tamale with his own three children and wife, in hopes of getting Carlos enrolled at a nearby Seventh Day Adventist school. Carlos said his parents had wanted him to stay at home to help with the family farm and the care of

Carlos Muta of Tamale, Ghana, my fourteen-year-old lookalike.
Courtesy, N'Kia Jones (Campbell).

younger siblings. His uncle, who sold handmade jewelry at the market and who hoped to attend university, however, had reasoned that if Carlos received an education, he would then be better able to assist his family.

"I'll help you, Carlos," I said. "I'll help you to go to school. You know, you look just like me!"

I dashed him some cedis (as a tip of kindness), exchanged mail and e-mail addresses, and then rushed onto the bus, waving at my newfound family member as we pulled away.

Having traveled halfway around the world, I had met a younger version of myself. Since arriving in Ghana, I'd seen numerous people who looked like members of my extended family—aunts, uncles, cousins—and community members. But meeting Carlos had been like staring into a mirror!

This phenomenon repeated itself almost a year later in Sierra Leone. Moments after stepping off the airplane at Lungi Airport on May 26, 2005, as a participant in "Priscilla's Homecoming," a ceremoniously dressed Dr. Chernor A. Jalloh, Minister of Tourism & Culture, pulled me aside to confer quietly.

Dr. Chernor A. Jalloh, Minister of Tourism & Culture, my Sierra Leonean lookalike.
Photo by Lenny Spears.

With a twinkle of admiration in his eyes, Dr. Jalloh welcomed me and confided, "You look like my people. I am Fula. Anh-hanh. I saw you coming off the plane wearing your Ghana hat." He smiled and embraced me as though I was a long-lost relative, saying, "You are Fula!"

The photograph made of us the next day, standing side by side, is a cherished possession. In it, I am wearing a kente kofi and a green batik shirt I'd bought at a Ghanaian market. Dr. Jalloh is attired in a flowing white Sierra Leonean kaftan and hat with intricate embroidery. Unlike our clothing, our cheekbones, our physiques, our noses, our almond-shaped eyes, and our smiles match each other's detail for detail.

Throughout the week-long "Priscilla's Homecoming" celebration, whenever Dr. Jalloh saw me, he proclaimed, "Fula, I tell you! You are Fula!"

The Fulas are the largest and most geographically dispersed tribe in West Africa. They are primarily farmers and shepherds and are the largest speaking ethnic group in West Africa. Most are Muslim.

Memories of meeting Carlos Muta and Chenor Jalloh are stirring reminders of my connections with West Africa. "What a mighty God we serve . . .," my spirit sang to the tune of the old Gullah spiritual, as we each looked into eyes on faces seemingly molded by a sculptor whose signature styles we were modeling. "He didn't have to do it, but He did!"

That song reminds me of my connections with West Africa on another occasion. During a service at Our Lady Star of the Sea Catholic Church in Juba, Freetown, I heard a similar refrain as a mass choir sang melodious strains with African rhythms and harmonies. Before sharing a passage with them in Gullah from *De Good Nyews Wa John Write*, I implored the audience to sing with me a spiritual from my homeland that sounded so much like a song they had sung. To be baptized in the syncopations of their musicians and the timbre of their choir members as I led this song, I imagined, would bring ecstacy divine. The result was rapturous—above and beyond what I had hoped for or expected! The choir members knew the song, and with tinges of Krio mixed with Gullah, we praised the Source who had connected all assembled for this event.

"It's good for us to be gathered in the same attire," the Reverend Father Ambrose M. Damba began his message. Looking into the audience, he viewed a sea of women in blue dresses stamped with "C.W.A." This service was the Catholic Women's Association Western Area 5th Annual Thanksgiving Mass and celebration of "Priscilla's Homecoming." "But our actions should go beyond our attire," Damba continued. "God wants us to form a community. God wants us to form a family."

My family and my wardrobe have grown since my visits to West Africa, and I desire my actions to go beyond my attire of West African outfits. I'm hopeful that Dr. Jalloh will find my writings a boon to the Sierra Leone Ministry of Tourism and Culture. I'm expectant that Carlos will graduate and assist others. To date, he has advanced to junior secondary school, or middle school, having begun as a fourth grader in 2004 when I assumed sponsoring his education. I've dubbed him my "Ghanaian son," and he calls me "Dad." He hopes, he tells me, to one day be Ghana's president!

On September 14, 2006, I read my DNA analysis as reported by African Ancestry, Inc. (www.africanancestry.com) and learned that my visits to Ghana and Sierra Leone had been more of a family reunion than I realized! Although I'm not Fula, as Dr. Jalloh proclaimed, I share maternal genetic ancestry with the Temne people living in Sierra Leone. And Carlos and I could be long-lost relatives indeed, as I share paternal genetic ancestry with the Ewe and Akan peoples in Ghana.

That I've traveled to the countries of my ancestry on my first two visits to Africa is astounding! My response whenever I contemplate the odds of this occurrence is "**What a mighty God we serve!**"

"What A Mighty God We Serve"

(Gullah spiritual)

What a mighty God we serve.
What a mighty God we serve.
He woke me up this morning, started me on my way.
What a mighty God we serve.

He didn't have to do it, but He did.
He didn't have to do it, but He did.
He woke me up this morning, started me on my way.
What a mighty God we serve.

He gives me strength from day to day.
He gives me strength from day to day.
He woke me up this morning, started me on my way.
What a mighty God we serve.

He gives me joy and gives me peace.
He gives me joy and gives me peace.
He woke me up this morning, started me on my way.
What a mighty God we serve.

He fills me with the breath of life.
He fills me with the breath of life.
He woke me up this morning, started me on my way.
What a mighty God we serve.

What a mighty God we serve.
What a mighty God we serve.
He woke me up this morning, started me on my way.
What a mighty God we serve.

De ol sheep done know de road.
De young lam mus fin de way.

In *Little Muddy Waters, A Gullah Folk Tale* (Daise 1989), a hard-headed little boy learns from his Gullah grandmother the importance of respecting one's elders. In Gullah communities, as handed down from African ancestors, respect for elders is a value no adult or child dare violate. In fact, for a child to disrespect an elder is regarded as a mark of being void of the spirit of God.

The book's main character has been given the basket name Little Muddy Waters because of his dark complexion. Despite his good looks and home-training, he disrespects, sasses, and lies to an elder, Ol Man Weava, who responds, "So you don't know to respect yo elders, huh?" and then puts "de mout" on the impudent child. Weava closes one eye, points a finger at the boy and curses him, shouting, "Why you ent nottin. You ent come from nottin. And if this day don't bring a good change in you, you ent gon mount to nottin. Mark my word!"

Raised to fear repercussions from having "de mout" railed against them, Gullah children are constantly reminded in words reminiscent of Grandma Waters' admonition: "Respect yo elders and do what's right." During my visits to Ghana and Sierra Leone, I saw many boys who, like Little Muddy Waters, were "dark and dashing just like an African prince." Many, also like Little Muddy Waters, had a space between their two top front teeth. In Gullah communities, that space is tagged "De Liar's Gap" and signifies that the individual fabricates compulsively. I learned while in West Africa, however, that having "de Gap" is a mark of beauty and sensuality, as observed in other communities of the African Diaspora. Through the years, Gullah beliefs about this physical feature somehow got twisted. I conjecture that perhaps this occurred because those pursued consistently by flatterers and prospective paramours had to resort to lying in order to create distance and raise boundaries.

In Ghana and Sierra Leone I saw children of all ages and genders who were—at all times—respectful to elders. The sight was astonishing!

At Tuwohofo-Holly International School in Akotokyir Village in Cape Coast, Ghana, students remained attentive throughout the school day even though they sat in crowded cinder block classrooms with dirt floors. They woke early, toted water from wells or rivers to their homes, swept the ground in their yards with hand brooms and performed other chores, then dressed in brown school uniforms and walked . . . *miles* . . . to school. Students took notes on paper or in paper handbooks that teachers collected daily because in Ghana paper is a luxury. Waste baskets in classrooms were non-existent; nothing was wasted! Pencils were a rarity. Pens were used. And teachers wrote on slate boards that had no ledges for holding chalk.

Ventilation was from windows without glass or screens—just openings. When goats and chickens meandered into classrooms, the education-at-hand didn't lose a beat. When clapping or singing erupted from nearby classrooms that were separated by walls that didn't extend fully to the ceiling, students focused only on whatever lesson was going on. Few, if any, disruptions occurred. There were no textbooks, no electricity, no modern conveniences in the

Female Ghanaian school students wear close-cropped hair throughout high school.
Photo by author.

Photos courtesy,
Don Clerico, Charleston
Southern University.

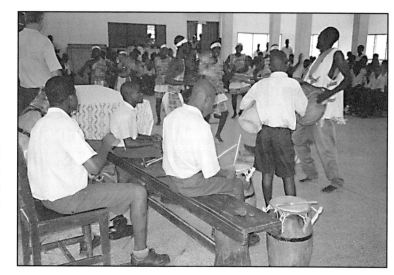

Blind drummers and deaf dancers at Cape Deaf School in Cape Coast, Ghana, perform with precision and panache.

Seven dancers of School of African Rhythm and Dance in Cape Coast, Ghana, perform the award-winning dance in which females blow ram's horns. Prior to its debut, it had been taboo for females to blow horns, following the belief that doing so would cause infertility.

village schools. Girls didn't apply makeup or fix their do's while in classes. In fact, all Ghanaian girl students wear their hair cut short until they graduate. Boys didn't disrupt classes by cracking jokes or fussing and fighting. Teachers hardly ever raised their voices for students to behave.

In short, students knew to "respect their elders and do what's right."

Students at Cape Deaf School, also in Cape Coast, modeled respectfulness and self-dignity 24:7. With unparalleled precision and excellence, blind drummers and deaf dancers of the School of African Rhythm and Dance (SARD), the school's performance troupe, compelled me to sit in awe as I watched them and to dance with joy as I listened to them.

Mr. Cooper, the drumming instructor, said his work at Cape Deaf School is to show handicapped students that not only can they excel at drumming but at anything they attempt. The school's motto is "Disability—Not Inability."

Mrs. Letitia Mensah, founder of SARD, stated that she endeavors to bridge the gap between the blind and the deaf so they would know that all things are possible. The troupe has won the prestigious National Award for Performance, the top award granted in South Africa, because of a dance choreographed by Mrs. Mensah in which seven female dancers blew ram's horns. Prior to that performance, it had been considered taboo for females to blow horns. It was believed that if females blew any horns, they would not be able to conceive babies. However, the dance broke the tradition, and the taboo was proven false.

Throughout Ghanaian history, whenever kings or chiefs traveled, seven male horn blowers preceded them to herald their arrival. In respect for this revered custom, the country's memorial to President Kwame Nkrumah includes seven wooden horn blowers kneeling elegantly before Nkrumah's large statue.

In addition to performing arts, students at Cape Deaf School also study academic subjects, as well as courses in batik, wood carving, sewing, and moral and religious education. Additionally, they work the gardens and feed the animals from which they get their food supply.

These students exude a sense of self-confidence evident in the Gullah people portrayed in *Reminiscences of Sea Island Heritage*. The children's work ethic and independent spirit mirrors that of freed slaves who attended Penn School on St. Helena Island, the school from which my parents graduated and Penn Center evolved.

In Sierra Leone, scores of uniformed school children lined the roadside approaching Dunkeba Village during "Priscilla's Homecoming." Over and over again, they sang the verse of a Sierra Leonean folk song in honor of Thomalind Martin Polite's arrival:

> Home again, I ask you; home again, I ask you
> When shall I see my home
> When shall I see my native land
> I shall never forget my home

Another group of Sierra Leonean students, sixth graders—all ten years old, like Priscilla when she was captured—researched, wrote, and performed a skit

Uniformed children in Dunkegba Village, Sierra Leone, singing "Home Again" to welcome Thomalind Martin Polite.
Courtesy, Jacque Metz.

Youths gathered at Tasso Island, Sierra Leone, to greet Thomalind Martin Polite during Priscilla's Homecoming. Photo by author.

School children peering through windows at Tuwohofo-Holly International School in Akotokyir Village, Cape Coast, Ghana.
Courtesy, Don Clerico, Charleston Southern University.

about Sierra Leonean female heroes. These included physicians, attorneys, educators, traditional chiefs, and others. The students discovered these characters' stories in school textbooks and through oral history; immersed themselves in their struggles, disappointments, and visions; and shared them with an appreciative audience gathered at Freetown's Light House Restaurant to commemorate "Priscilla's Homecoming." To conclude the performance, one student asked poignantly, "Priscilla, had you not been taken away from us, which one of these great women would you have become?"

The discipline and productivity I witnessed among West African children, despite their lack of material abundance, was a by-product of an age-old value handed down to Gullah descendants: de ol sheep done know de road, an de young lam mus fin de way.

Ron teaches students at Tuwohofo-Holly International School in Akotokyir Village in Cape Coast, Ghana. Courtesy, Don Clerico, Charleston Southern University.

"De Ol Sheep Done Know de Road"

(Gullah spiritual, from *Reminiscences of Sea Island Heritage*)

De ol sheep done kno de road.
De ol sheep done kno de road.
De ol sheep done know de road.
De young lam mus fin de way.
De young lam mus fin de way.

Shout, my brotha, you are free!
  De young lam mus fin de way.
Christ has brought your liberty!
  De young lam mus fin' de way.

De ol sheep done know de road.
De ol sheep done know de road.
De ol sheep done know de road.
De young lam mus fin de way.
De young lam mus fin de way.

Fight, my brotha, don't you run!
  De young lam mus fin' de way.
Don't go away til de battle is won!
  De young lam mus fin de way.

De ol sheep done know de road.
De ol sheep done know de road.
De ol sheep done know de road.
De young lam mus fin de way.
De young lam mus fin de way.

Good Lord, I done done.
I done done what You tol me ta do.

The following lesson about diversity of cultural mores, "Pageantry: Ghanaian Festivals & Celebrations," was developed as a follow-up to the "Teaching and Learning in Ghana 2004" program, funded through Charleston Southern University. Excerpts of creative arts activities illustrate the diversity of cultural mores in Ghana today and may be adapted for use in grades 4 through 10. The "TLG 2004 Ghana-Related Lessons & Curricula" (and the complete "Pageantry: Ghanaian Festivals & Celebrations" lesson) are accessible on-line at www.csuniv.edu/ghana/index.asp.

SOUTH CAROLINA CURRICULUM STANDARDS:
• Read a variety of texts fluently.
• Develop an extended response around a central idea, using relevant supporting details.
• Revise writing for clarity, vocabulary, and effective phrasing through collaboration and self-evaluation.
• Use language, vocabulary appropriate for the purpose and audience. Face an audience, make eye contact, use the appropriate voice level, gestures, facial expressions, and posture when making oral presentations.

NOTE TO TEACHERS:
"Pageantry: Ghanaian Festivals & Celebrations" is designed to examine common cultural and societal mores, such as naming practices, marriage customs, funeral traditions, and day-to-day practices. This study will engage students to understand and appreciate their own individual mores as well as those of classmates. Simultaneously, it will examine Ghanaian customs and traditions, which define the uniqueness of a people who celebrate life and freedom.

PAGEANTRY: GHANAIAN FESTIVALS & CELEBRATIONS

Ghanaian Lineage

Read to students the following information about Ghanaian culture, from *A Handbook on Ghanaian Culture* by Osei Kwadwo. Instruct the students to be prepared afterward to answer questions and complete activities.

> Ghanaians learn early to use their heads—for physical as well as intellectual purposes. Toddlers will mimic the practices of parents or older siblings, but at about age 6 they will begin toting objects on their heads as an early lesson in responsibility. Girls carry firewood, foodstuffs, and water. Boys will also carry water, crops, and tools. In adulthood, ladies will tote items for vending in the marketplace or foodstuffs for using in meals. Men carry wood, and lumber for the roofing of houses or bundles of grass for thatched roofs.
>
> The Asante people of Ghana are part of a greater society called the Akan Society. Other tribes in Ghana that belong to the Akan Society are: the Akyems, Bonos, Kwahus, Assins, Fantes, Sefwis, Denkyiras, Wassas, Akwamus and Akwapims. All Akan people believe in the existence of God, the Creator.
>
> Akans belong to Matrilineal clans. Accordingly, children's positions in society and inheritance are traced through the mother's line. It is believed that members of any Akan clan or tribe are all related, regardless of their geographical distance from each other. They are regarded as brothers and sisters and, therefore, cannot marry among themselves. (p. ix-v)
>
> The administrative hierarchy in towns and villages follows this order: The chief is the head. He is supported by the elders who are selected from the different clans of the town. The clan elders form the next in command and are followed by the heads-of-families. These are followed by house elders and then ordinary citizens. (p. 120)

Have students answer the following questions:
1. What are some responsibilities Ghanaian children begin learning at age six?
2. What responsibilities did you begin at age six or earlier? What values have those responsibilities taught you?
3. What responsibilities will you begin to teach your children at an early age? The same ones you learned from your parents/guardians? Or new ones?
4. What values do you think are important for children to have? Why?
5. Will you instruct your children to befriend but not marry any kind of people? Any group of people? Why?
6. Who is regarded as the chief elder in your family? Is he/she so honored because of age? Reputation? Particular ability? Are you close to this individual? What advice has he/she given you?

Answers:
1. Boys carry water and crops. Girls carry firewood, foodstuffs, and water.

Child Naming Practices

Read the following information to students as an introduction to Child Naming Practices.

> According to Akan custom, the prerogative of naming a child is vested in the father only. The mother has no right in naming a child when the father is present. Even if the father dies before the baby is born, the successor of the father is consulted for a name for the baby. (Kwadwo, 37)

Have students read pages 33–36 of *A Handbook on Asante Culture*.

Have students answer the following questions:
1. Years ago in Asante culture, what was believed to be the cause of difficulty during childbirth?
2. What are some medically proven causes for difficulty during childbirth?
3. When does child naming take place? How did this custom start?
4. According to Akan custom, who first tells the baby its name? What else would the child be told?

5. Who named you? What does your name mean? If you don't know the meaning of your name, what do you think it should mean? Why?

6. Why would an infant be told, "If you taste water, call it water" and "If you taste wine, call it wine"?

7. What have you been told were the first words said to you following your birth? What would you like to think were the very first words you heard?

8. What do you think will be the first words you tell your children? Why?

9. What kinds of persons would Akan parents refrain from naming children after? Why?

10. What would your Ghanaian given name be if you were born on:

    Sunday _____   Tuesday _____   Friday _____
    Monday _____   Wednesday _____   Saturday _____
                           Thursday _____

11. What would be the given name of someone of your opposite sex who was born on:

    Sunday _____   Tuesday _____   Friday _____
    Monday _____   Wednesday _____   Saturday _____
                           Thursday _____

12. In addition to being assigned names because of the day of birth, what other occurrences could contribute to a child's naming?

Answers:
1. A woman's unfaithfulness to her husband.
2. Reasons include improper prenatal care, genetic defects, position of the baby in the birth canal, and a genetic predisposition.
3. On the eighth day following bith. It was believed that if a baby survived up to one week, it had come to stay.
4. The elderly woman of the house. She would narrate the good deeds of the person the child was named after and would urge the infant to emulate that person.
5. Answers will vary.
6. To imply that the infant should always speak the truth.
7. Answers will vary.
8. Answers will vary.
9. A lazy person, a thief, a murderer, a rapist, or a person of questionable character because the baby would grow up and copy the characters of these individuals.
10. Answers will vary.

11. (Male names)

Sunday:	Kwesi	Tuesday:	Kwabina	Friday:	Afua
Monday:	Kwodwo	Wednesday:	Ekua	Saturday:	Ama
		Thursday:	Yaw		

(Female names)

Sunday:	Akousa	Tuesday:	Abena	Friday:	Afia
Monday:	Adwoa	Wednesday:	Akua	Saturday:	Amma
		Thursday:	Yaa		

12. Happenings or situations, festive days, deities, important days, child's features or place of birth.

Marriage Customs

Have students read aloud the information below about marriage in Ghanaian culture. Inform students to be prepared afterward to answer questions and complete activities.

Marriage is one of the important pillars upon which the Asante culture rests. The other important pillars are the clan system, beliefs of the people, and the structure of government. From time immemorial, marriage has been a sacred union that bound two people together. The Asantes look at marriage as union between two lovers, a male and a female, which naturally becomes the union of two or four clans, i.e., the union between a man and his wife and the union between the parents of the man and the parents of the woman.

Sometimes marriages join tribes together. For example, if an Asante man marries a Ga woman, this marriage binds the two tribes together because anything that happens in either tribe, that of the man or of the woman, affects the two tribes. If the man is bereaved, the in-laws from the Ga tribe would be involved, as it would be if or when something happens in the woman's tribe. The man and his people are affected since they have to go to the help of the woman's people.

If a man dies, his wife is given to a relative to marry so that this new man could look after the children the husband left. But if a woman dies, a substitute is not given to the husband. When a "stool" wife (wife of a chief who sits on a stool, or throne) dies, somebody is selected from her house to succeed her and marry the chief. If a chief is destooled, his stool wives can choose to go with him or divorce him and marry the new chief who has been enstooled.

Some marriages are frowned upon by Ghanaians, though they are not against the law. Such marriages include:

- a man and his sister marrying a woman and her brother
- a man marrying a woman who is far older than he.

But if a man marries a woman far younger than he, it is interpreted that the man has lived a respectable life and that is why a younger woman has agreed to marry him.

With the mixture of cultures to Asante culture, western-influenced weddings, Christian weddings, and Muslim weddings have become commonplace. Traditional Asante marriage rituals are taught in Ghanaian schools as part of a government-mandated Moral and Religious Education curriculum component. Although English is the official language in Ghana, these classes are taught in the traditional language or dialect of each community (Kwadwo, 21–22). This is done so that students develop a sound moral attitude and a healthy appreciation of cultural heritage.

The qualities of marriage (*awargye*) include that the groom

(a) should be of good character,

(b) should be a productive worker,

(c) should not be a womanizer,

(d) should not be lazy,

(e) should not be impotent, and

(f) should not be a drunkard.

In order to pursue marriage, a couple must follow many cultural steps. The prospective bride and groom must first consult their parents. The parents will then consult the candidates' uncles for consent. Omitting this step could potentially lead to family disharmony. For example, if a bride or groom falls into hardship and subsequently seeks assistance from the family, an uncle whose consent had not been sought, as well as his family, might respond, "I did not know you were married" [even if this was not the case]. By custom, he would not be obligated to help.

Should the uncles consent, and the parents also, each family then sends an emissary to the other family to ask permission. The response will be, "I don't know." Each family would then conduct investigations about the marriage candidates' health issues, character, etc.

The groom's family will accompany him with gifts—money, cows, drinks, etc.—for the bride's family and assist him in providing the following essential monetary gifts:

(a) *ztsinsa* — dowry paid to the bride's family

(b) *tambobaa* — money paid to the bride's mother to show that the bride has brought respect to her family; the mother's gift must be the most substantial

(c) *bowdotoa* — money paid to the bride's parents to compensate for the suffering they endured during her birth

(d) *tsirade* — a substantial amount of money given to the bride so that she can establish herself

(e) *akontansekan* — money paid to the brothers of the bride because she will be taken away from them

(f) *ehyiadze* — money given to the bride to purchase tam (clothes), *mpboa* (sandals), *ahwehwe* (mirror), and *adaka* (special bag or pocketbook)

(g) *nkwansanbue* — money so that the bride can purchase ingredients to prepare the first meal for her husband. (The bride MUST take time in preparing this meal so that the husband will enjoy it.)

Acceptance for the marriage, if given by the bride's family, will be stated in the presence of both families.

Following these customs ensures that the bride and groom are properly married according to cultural and societal mandates. Spiritual blessings or confirmation may or may not be given; however, the couple may from that moment live together as husband and wife.

If a church wedding occurs, it must follow these cultural dictates and may take place years later or even after children have been born to the union. Many couples postpone or choose not to have a formal wedding because such events are costly, involving feeding and entertaining enormous crowds from both families and tribes. Many elect to build a home instead.

Have students answer the following questions:
1. Why are traditional Asante marriage rituals taught to students only in the traditional language or dialect of the community and not in English?
2. What conditions of marriage are frowned upon by Ghanaians?
3. What conditions of marriage do you frown upon? Why?
4. Identify three qualities of *awargye*.
5. Which two qualities of *awargye* do you agree with most? Why? What quality or qualities would you add?
6. Which gift of a Ghanaian groom do you find the most unusual? Why?
7. If one gift-giving custom of Ghanaian culture were adopted in your culture, which gift would you wish to keep? Why?
8. Have students role-play the qualities of *awargye*. (A female could explain to others why she suspects an interested suitor is not a good catch. A male could discuss with others why he knows he will be considered well by an admirer).

Answers:
1. To teach students to develop a healthy appreciation of cultural heritage.
2. A man and his sister marrying a woman and her brother; a man marrying a significantly older woman
3. Answers will vary.
4. Groom should be of good character and a productive worker, and *not* a womanizer, lazy, impotent, or a drunkard.
5. Answers will vary.
6. Answers will vary.
7. Answers will vary.

Day-to-Day Practices

Have students read aloud the following list of day-to-day Ghanaian practices:
• Limbs are placed on paved or dirt roadways to give notice that a broken vehicle is ahead, either on the road or shoulder.
• Only goats, cattle, and chickens are given right-of-way by drivers; pedestrians may walk close to the roadway, but drivers will toot, then hit.
• If a driver hits a pedestrian or cyclist, he/she must drive the injured to the hospital or an angry mob will surround the accident until the driver does so.

- Before a public enstoolment, a chief must place his buttocks on his stool three times in the secrecy of his home. No woman is allowed to see the stool before the ceremony.
- For a chief to be destooled, he must have his stool taken from under him three times, his sandals must be removed and used to hit him on his head three times.
- Persons in line to be chief must be trained in manners and diplomacy.
- Only the linguist, the spokesman, may speak to or for the chief. People must address only the linguist.
- Speed bumps on paved roads, called "rumble ridges," are usually in sets of threes.
- Ghanaian business owners affirm their spirituality in the names of their businesses (e.g., Almighty Motors, Give It to God Food Stand, Lord Our Banner Auto Parts, Only God Can Judge Fashion Shop, and Great Provider Boutique).
- Following a heavy rain, village children along a dirt roadway will shovel dirt into the gullies and accept a "dash," or tip, from drivers (who probably would not have been able to pass without their assistance).
- In order to get attention in a public gathering, someone will call loudly, "Ago-o-o-o." Listeners will acknowledge by responding, "A-me-e-n!"
- At funerals, family members of the deceased dress in red.
- The following plants and herbs are boiled for medicinal purposes: nim tree leaves (malaria); baobab tree leaves (stomach pain and diarrhea); silk cotton tree leaves (colds); mango tree leaves (stomach pain); and a combination of mango, nim, and ebony tree leaves (impotency).
- Ghanaians are mindful of the following taboos (in fear of dreadful consequences): not to disrespect elders, not to farm on Sunday, not to sing while bathing, not to sing while eating, not to go to sea on Tuesday, not to whistle in the evening.

Have students select two day-to-day cultural practices. In groups of three or four, have students discuss their interpretations of how or why the practice started, how the practice differs in our country, and if and why they would maintain any aspect of the Ghanaian practice. Have each group report its answers to the class.

<u>Being Ghanaian</u>

Have students read Ghana's Department of Tourism's seven-sentence "Statement of Identity," written by Dinah Amely Ayensu. Inform them that the statement is displayed throughout the country on posters featuring a colorfully dressed and smiling Ghanaian woman.

> To be Ghanaian
> — is to have a sense of belonging
>   and a sense of family
> — is to be educated and disciplined
> — is to have a healthy body
> — is to be filled with a sense of loyalty
> — is to be united in spite of our ethnicity
> — is to have an awareness
>   of our African culture and tradition
> — is to be
>   Hospitable.

Point out to students that the concluding line supports a point of view boasted by Ghanaians young and old: **Ghana is the friendliest country in Africa!**

Have students write a five- to seven-sentence "statement of identity" about their family, community, or country. Like Dinah Amely Ayensu in her statement about Ghana, each should begin with "To be a [use family, town, or country name here]" and conclude with a statement that most capably captures their thoughts about the subject. Encourage students to read their writings to classmates.

REFERENCE:
A Handbook on Asante Culture by Osei Kwadwo. O Kwadwo Enterprise, Ghana 2002. ISBN 9988-7596-5-7.

"Good Lord, I Done Done"

(Gullah spiritual, from *Reminiscences of Sea Island Heritage*)

Good Lord, I done done;
Good Lord, I done done;
Good Lord, I done done;
I done done what You tol' me to do.

You aks me to love, an' I done that, too.
You aks me to love, an' I done that, too.
You aks me to love, an' I done that, too.
I done done what You tol' me to do.

Good Lord, I done done;
Good Lord, I done done;
Good Lord, I done done;
I done done what You tol' me to do.

You aks me to pray, an' I done that, too.
You aks me to pray, an' I done that, too.
You aks me to pray, an' I done that, too.
I done done what You tol' me to do.

Good Lord, I done done;
Good Lord, I done done;
Good Lord, I done done;
I done done what You tol' me to do.

You aks me to sing, an' I done that, too.
You aks me to sing, an' I done that, too.
You aks me to sing, an' I done that, too.
I done done what You tol' me to do.

Good Lord, I done done;
Good Lord, I done done;
Good Lord, I done done;
I done done what You tol' me to do.

"The Golden Smile"

The smile of Ghanaian children
is golden.
It glitters with self-dignity
and sparkles
in response to the call of parents and grandparents, which proclaims:
"People may not be rich,
but they don't allow the pressures of life
to overwhelm them"
and
"`Sankofa' ~ which means 'Go back to your roots'"
and
"Do not forget
Pikworo ~ 'Place of the Rocks'
Salaga Slave Camp
Elmina Castle's 'Door of No Return.'"

Courtesy, Don Clerico, Charleston Southern University.

The smile of Ghanaian children,
in its crudest and even most refined forms,
shimmeringly stabilizes
the values of
freedom, tolerance and unity
as taught by Ghana's historical and cultural icons ~
President Kwame Nkrumah, W.E.B. DuBois, King Prempeh.

Photos courtesy, Don Clerico,
Charleston Southern University.

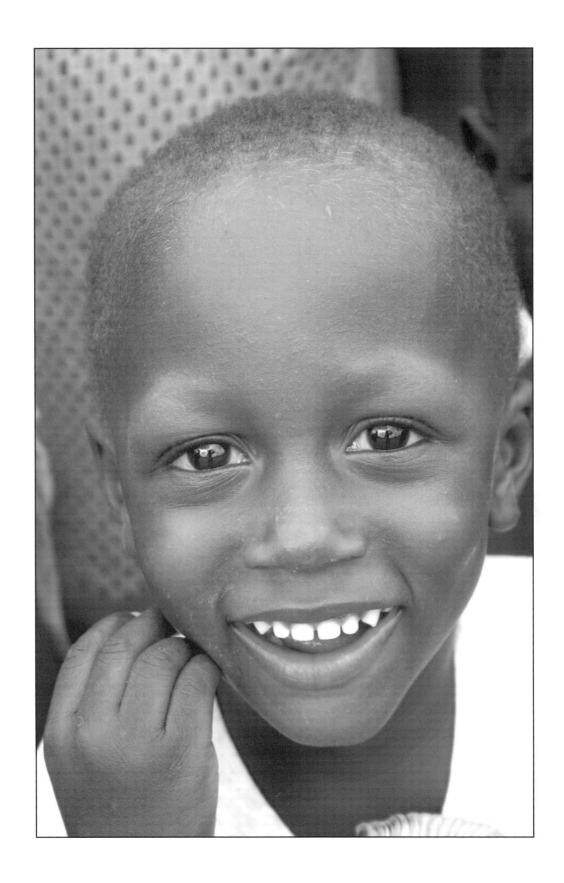

It is as unique and beautiful
as the bounty of Ghana's forests
and the crafts of its artisans
who showcase
regal Kente cloth,
mesmerizing Batik,
intricate carvings of wood ~
the smile of Ghanaian children.
It is as priceless
as the mineral wealth of their nation,
which adorns the world.
As alluring
as the laughter of children—
girls, stomping, clapping
in the hand-game Ampe
and
boys, kicking, scoring
in soccer.
As valuable and as celebrated
as Ananse stories
and
as full of pageantry as festivals.

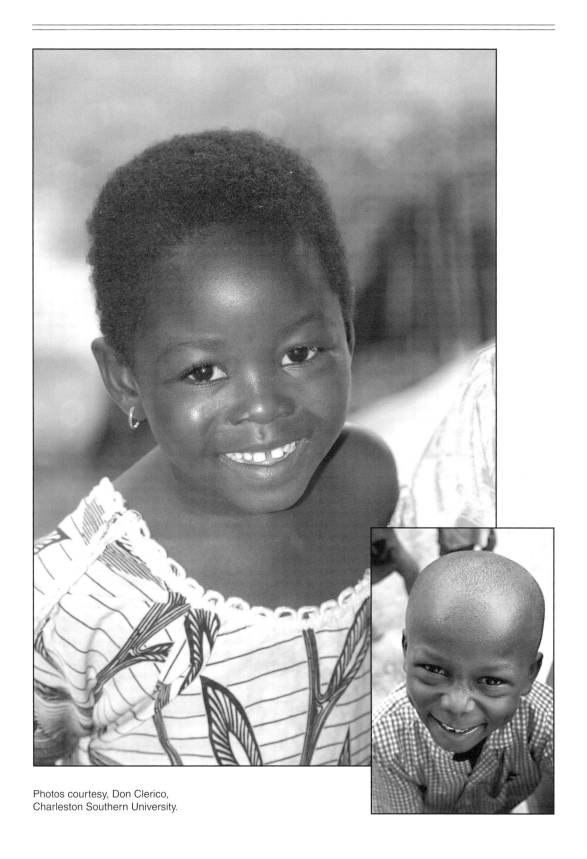

Photos courtesy, Don Clerico,
Charleston Southern University.

A smile,
a simple smile
flashed as mundanely as Ghanaian men and women
balance bundles and baskets on their heads,
speaks wisdom
as stirring and joyous
as
voices,
united,
extol the National Anthem:
"God bless our homeland Ghana,
And make our nation great and strong,
Bold to defend for ever
The cause of Freedom and of Right;
Fill our hearts with true humility,
Make us cherish fearless honesty,
And help us to resist oppressors' rule
With all our will and might for evermore."

Photos courtesy,
Don Clerico, Charleston
Southern University.

Ghana's Blackstar
molds
the smile of Ghanaian children
to represent
hope,
radiant and undying.
It is smelted
by education
in Village homes and schools
and
in private and public schools, when possible.
Its stamp of purity
is an inner
seal of self-determination:

"I will help my Village."
"I will bring honor to my family."
"I can do it."
"I will."

The smile of Ghanaian children
is
golden.

Photos courtesy, Don Clerico, Charleston Southern University.

I'm standing on a Rock that will never give away.

   I developed this descriptive writing lesson, "Layered Meanings; Multiple Truths," as a follow-up to the "Teaching and Learning in Ghana 2004" program, funded through Charleston Southern University. It interprets the poem "The Golden Smile" and offers several guided lessons on figurative language, which may be adapted for use in grades 5–12. The "TLG 2004 Ghana-Related Lessons & Curricula" are accessible on-line at www.csuniv.edu/ghana/index.asp.

SOUTH CAROLINA CURRICULUM STANDARDS:

<u>Reading Process and Comprehension</u>
* 8-R1.1   Demonstrate the ability to read a variety of texts fluently
* 8-R2.6   Demonstrate the ability to analyze and interpret figurative language
* 8-R2.7   Demonstrate the ability to identify imagery and symbolism
* 8-R2.9   Demonstrate the ability to identify elements of poetry such as rhyme, scheme, refrain, stanza
* 8-R2.10 Demonstrate the ability to identify the author's purpose in texts in a variety of genres

<u>Communication: Speaking</u>
* 8-C1.1   Demonstrate the ability to use language, vocabulary, and presentation techniques appropriate for the purpose and audience
* 8-C1.2   Demonstrate the ability to express and explain ideas orally, with fluency and confidence
* 8-C1.3   Demonstrate the ability to participate in conversations and discussions by responding appropriately
* 8-C1.6   Demonstrate the ability to present dramatic readings of literary selections
* 8-C1.9   Demonstrate the ability to use Standard American English (SAE) in formal speaking situations and in the classroom
* 8-C1.11 Demonstrate the ability to make appropriate statements to communicate agreement or disagreement with the ideas of others

- 8-C1.12 Demonstrate the ability to analyze and refine varied presentations through collaboration, conferencing, and self-evaluation
- 8-C1.15 Demonstrate the ability to use critical analysis to formulate appropriate oral responses

Communication: Listening
- 8-C2.1 Demonstrate the ability to listen for meaning in conversations and discussions

The Writing Process
- 8-W1.2 Demonstrate the ability to generate drafts that use a logical progression of ideas to develop a topic for a specific audience and/or purpose
- 8-W1.4 Demonstrate the ability to revise writing for clarity, sentence variety, precise vocabulary, and effective phrasing through collaboration, conferencing, and self-evaluation
- 8-W1.5 Demonstrate the ability to edit language convection such as spelling, capitalization, punctuation, agreement, sentence structure (syntax), and word usage
- 8-W2.2 Demonstrate the ability to use writing to learn, entertain, and describe

Responding to Text
- 8-W3.1 Demonstrate the ability to respond to texts both orally and in writing
- 8-W3.2 Demonstrate the ability to use literary models to refine his or her own writing
- 8-W3.3 Demonstrate the ability to use texts to make connections and support ideas in his or her own writing

NOTE TO TEACHERS:

The readings and activities in "Layered Meanings; Multiple Truths" are designed to help students identify, analyze, and use figurative writing. As emphasized in the poem "The Golden Smile," students will incorporate the literary elements of similes, metaphors, and extended metaphors to explore their understanding and appreciation of family, culture, and nationality. Individual writing, followed by presentations and group discussions, will foster acceptance of what individual students may find significant about each topic.

The greatest compliment I have received about the "The Golden Smile" was given by the Ghanaian tour guide for the TLG 2004 program: "You are a great writer! You have so movingly captured everything that I've tried to show you." I hope students, likewise, will capture the joy, enthusiasm, and appreciation of who they are and where they come from.

LAYERED MEANINGS; MULTIPLE TRUTHS

Activity A

Have students read the poem "The Golden Smile." (See page 89.)

Discuss the meanings of **metaphor** and **simile.** Metaphors and similes are integral to descriptive and creative writing.

- A **metaphor** is a literary element in which two things are compared. FOR EXAMPLE: My vacation was a rainbow, colorful and inspiring.
- A **simile** is a literary element in which two things are compared, using *like* or *as*. FOR EXAMPLE: My textbook, *like* my first book of nursery rhymes, doesn't get opened anymore.

Have students write sentences using **metaphor**s for the following words or phrases:

1. best friend _____

2. telephone _____

3. favorite pair of shoes _____

4. pet _____

5. grandparent _____

Have students write sentences using **simile**s for the following words or phrases:

1. memory _____

2. photo book _____

3. favorite family vacation _____

4. Christmas holidays _____

5. bedroom _____

Discuss **extended metaphors**. An extended metaphor prolongs a comparison throughout an entire literary piece. Read "Mother to Son" by Langston Hughes.

"Mother to Son"

Well, son, I'll tell you:
Life for me ain't been no crystal stair.
It's had tacks in it,
And splinters
And boards torn up,
And places with no carpet on the floor—
Bare.
But all the time
I'se been a climin' on,
And reachin' landin's,
And turnin' corners,
And sometimes goin' in the dark
Where there ain't been no light.
So, boy, don't you turn back.
Don't you set down on the steps
'Cause you find it's kinder hard.
Don't you fall now—
For I'se still goin', honey,
I'se still climbin',
And life for me ain't been no crystal stair.

Have students complete the following questions:

- Hughes compares life to a _____. He extends the comparison by stating that life, like a stairway, has what conditions?

  _____   _____

  _____   _____

- Hughes says that the mother, as though climbing a stairway, is still performing what actions of life?

  _____   _____

  _____   _____

Activity B

Have students re-read "The Golden Smile" and answer the following questions:

- What two things are being compared?

  _____ and _____

- Identify at least 10 ways the comparison is extended and identify the lines in the poem where the extended metaphors occur.

  1. *glitters – line 4*   6. _____
  2. _____   7. _____
  3. _____   8. _____
  4. _____   9. _____
  5. _____ 10. _____

Activity C

Have students identify a metaphor or simile for their family, nationality, or cultural group and complete the following activities:

- In complete sentences, list 5 to 10 reasons for your choice.
- Write a free-verse poem of at least 10 lines or a well-developed paragraph in which you extend your comparison. Remember to title your work.

Activity D

Have students discuss aspects of their own culture that they admire and dislike. Have them discuss and list topics in "The Golden Smile" they are unsure of and want to learn more about. Encourage them to become pen pals with students from Tuwohofo-Holly International School, visited by the developers of the "Layered Meanings; Multiple Truths" curriculum unit. Remind students to be sensitive to the fact that students in Akotokyir Village in Cape Coast, Ghana, may not be able to understand the abundance of material possessions American children enjoy, and the friendships that develop should be maintained.

Letters should be collected from the entire class and mailed to:

Mr. Ato Baidoo, Headmaster
Box AD 240
Tuwohofo-Holly International School
Cape Coast, Ghana, West Africa

In the cover letter to Mr. Baidoo, explain your class's purposes for establishing a pen pal relationship. Also, state that your participation is resulting from a curriculum written by Ronald Daise from the 2004 Teaching & Learning in Ghana program.

ANSWER KEY:
Activity A:
(Conditions)
Crystal stair
Had tacks in it
Had splinters in it
Had boards torn up
Bare

(Actions)
Been a climbin' on
Reachin' landin's
Turnin' corners'
Goin' in the dark where there ain't been no light

Activity B:

smile of a Ghanaian child and gold sparkles — line 5

shimmers — line 20

unique and beautiful — line 25

priceless — line 34

alluring — line 36

valuable and celebrated — line 43

flashes — line 43

smelted — line 71

stamped — line 76

"Standing on a Solid Rock"
(Gullah spiritual, from *Reminiscences of Sea Island Heritage*)

I'm standing on a solid rock
I'm standing on a solid rock
I'm standing on a rock that will never give away
I'm standing on a solid rock

I'm praying on a solid rock
I'm praying on a solid rock
I'm praying on a rock that will never give away
I'm praying on a solid rock

I'm teaching on a solid rock
I'm teaching on a solid rock
I'm teaching on a rock that will never give away
I'm teaching on a solid rock

I'm trusting in a solid rock
I'm trusting in a solid rock
I'm trusting in a rock that will never give away
I'm trusting in a solid rock

Jesus is that solid rock
King Jesus is that solid
Jesus is that rock that will never fade away
Jesus is that solid rock

Africa. West Africa.
Africa. West Africa.
There's a connection deep down in my spirit
With Africa. West Africa.

Love brought us here in Jesus name.

I began hearing old spirituals from my childhood as events unfolded during "Priscilla's Homecoming." Without prompting, tunes of songs that my African ancestors used to express their sorrows, joys, triumphs, and disappointments while working on South Carolina and Georgia plantations began to reverberate within my psyche, and I sang them softly or, more often, inaudibly. Other participants must have been amused as I bobbed my head, tapped my feet, or patted my hands on my thighs to some internal rhythm. Unbeknownst to them, I was hearing serenades of Gullah/Geechee rhythms that ancestral spirits were signaling my subconscious mind to utilize in chronicling my experiences with Gullah flavor.

This heavenly serenade began on day two, Friday, May 27. Thomalind Martin Polite, her husband Antawn, and "Priscilla's Posse"—the twenty-member entourage of organizers, film crew, scholars, journalists, book writers, and community representatives from South Carolina, Georgia, and Rhode Island—gathered to meet with Freetown's mayor Whitstanley Bankole-Johnson. Together with city officials, we squeezed tightly into seats around a large conference table. Enthusiastic Sierra Leonean community members stood and filled the room to overflowing. While awaiting the mayor's entrance, I recalled an old tune and began humming and tapping my feet as the reception unfolded:

> Well, I'm so glad I'm here
> So glad I'm here
> So glad I'm here in Jesus name
> Yes, I'm so glad I'm here
> So glad I'm here
> So glad I'm here in Jesus name

The Polites, ushered with Joseph Opala to the far end of the table, received excited glances and smiles from onlookers . . .

Let us sing while we're here
Sing while we're here
Sing while we're here in Jesus name
Let us sing while we're here
Sing while we're here
Sing while we're here in Jesus name

The chatter of pleasantries in Krio was songlike as Sierra Leoneans greeted Americans . . .

Let us pray while we're here
Pray while we're here
Pray while we're here in Jesus name
Let us pray while we're here
Pray while we're here
Pray while were' here in Jesus name

The ambiance, like what I believe will be sensed during the Great Coronation, made me feel as though I was in the presence of a heavenly delegation at the Second Coming . . .

You know Love brought us here
Love brought us here
Love brought us here in Jesus name
Love brought us here
Love brought us here
Love brought us here in Jesus name

Mayor Bankole-Johnson entered with aplomb, bearing a wooden mace and walking lord-like to the head of the table. Upon sitting, he expressed joy and admiration at the Polites' reconnecting with the heritage of their Sierra Leonean ancestor, Priscilla. He then spoke about trickster stories, with characters like Bra Spider, to acknowledge the links of Gullah and Sierra Leonean cultures and led a stirring Sierra Leonean spiritual, "Tell Am Tenki," in honor of the occasion:

Tel Am tenki, tel Am
Tel Papa Gohd tenki
Tel Am tenki, tel Am
Tell Papa Gohd tenki
Weytin I du foh mi

A go tel Am tenki
Weytin I du foh mi
A go tel Am tenki
Tel Am tenki, tel Am
Tel Papa Gohd tenki

According to Charlie Hafner, director of The Freetown Players, the premier cultural performance troupe of Sierra Leone, "Tel Am Tenki" is a direct Krio translation of "Tell Him Thank You" with "Am" referring to God. The English translation is:

Tell Him thank you, tell Him
Tell Papa God thank you
Tell Him thank you, tell Him
Tell Papa God thank you
What He did for me
I will tell Him (say) thank you
What He did for me
I will tell Him (say) thank you
Tell Him thank you, tell Him
Tell Papa God thank you
(Personal communication from Charlie Hafner, July 22, 2005, 9:27 AM)

Bankole-Johnson then asked if anyone present could express any other cultural similarities. All eyes around the conference table slowly turned to me, the "Priscilla's Homecoming" ambassador of Gullah culture. Because I had heard whisperings and syncopations of Gullah/Geechee rhythms only a few moments earlier, I stood, without pause, and jubilantly responded in song to the tune of the Gullah spiritual, "So Glad We Here in Jesus Name."

Well, I'm so glad we heh
So glad we heh
So glad we heh een Sierra Leone
Let we sing while we heh
Sing while we heh,
Sing while we heh een Sierra Leone

You know Gawd bring we heh
De Lawd bring we heh
De Sperit bring we heh ta Sierra Leone
We gon rejice while we heh

Clap an sing while we heh
We glad fa be heh een Sierra Leone

We greet de ancestas heh
We greet all de eldas heh
We greet Priscilla sperit heh een Sierra Leone
Thomalind glad fa be heh
Antawn glad fa be heh
We glad fa be heh een Sierra Leone

Words by Ronald Daise
© 2005

The cultural links of language, music, rhythm, and spirituality suffused the room. All sang, all clapped in unison, all realized we were one in purpose, one in heritage, one in family ties.

As the applause ebbed, Bankole-Johnson concluded, "I just had a feeling that there was something good pervading this house. And there was something I could gather to take me back to those Negro spirituals. These are songs we too sing here. We do it when we carry on wakes. And when we are happy. And when we tell stories."

Spirituals—songs of hope, songs with stories—masterfully, mesmerizingly, and within a matter of moments, had bridged the cultures of two continents.

An ebryboddy been tell Gawd "tenki" when dat meetin wit de Freetown Mayah been done!

Ron discusses the lyrics of "Tell Am Tenki" and sings with Priscilla's Homecoming members Valerie Tutson of Rhode Island (left), and Julliette Emmesiah and Marian Alfred of Sierra Leone.
Photo by Lenny Spears.

Well, I come this far, fin no fault, feel like journey on!

Gullah music has power! Call-and-response work songs and praise house shouts; coded message songs; spirituals of hope, determination, and faith; children's songs for games and learning all enable singers to journey on. Sometimes beginning, or ending, slowly with a plaintive moan or hum, the music's tempo can quicken, become polyrhythmic and energize hands and feet to become percussive, to fill in fully for African drumbeats that plantation owners long ago feared and prohibited. Gullah rhythms, clapped or tapped, are peculiar, hearkening back to West Africa yet maintaining a unique syncopation that can be identified solely as from the sea islands.

In my mind I heard a Gullah rhythm as Sierra Leone vice president Solomon Berewa addressed Thomalind Martin Polite and her husband Antawn at 9:00 AM, during the first full day of "Priscilla's Homecoming."

"This is the first time I am seeing in the flesh someone who is the family member of someone from Sierra Leone," he stated. Seated beside Thomalind and staring at her intently, he continued. "It is not just a fairy tale. It is something real indeed!

"In school we heard stories of people who were transported across the Atlantic to be slaves. We called them `the unfortunate.' But you are a sister returning after a long sojourn and having a bond established. This is something so real, something so true!

"I hope you feel the warmth of returning home. History is so alive! We are no longer separated by the Atlantic Ocean. It is the human connection that transcends everything. Welcome back to where we are—the home of your ancestors!"

Berewa's warm words and resplendent, baritone voice intrigued me as I scribbled notes. A former newspaper reporter, I intended to capture every moment of the historical, week-long adventure.

"This is something so real, something so true!" he had stated. Even as I continued writing, those words began to echo—no . . . *resound*—in my mind. Soon they became rhythmic. *Something so real, something so true! Something so real, something so true!*

Wrapped in a unique syncopation, peculiar, but hearkening back to West Africa, a song began to unfold on my notepad. Our crowded bus bustled through busy, narrow Freetown streets. I thought about pre-adolescent Priscilla and wrote. We stopped at a marketplace. Others shopped, but my mind found peace only by concentrating, scribbling, erasing, and rewriting. I left the merchants hawking colorful Sierra Leonean clothing, sparkling jewelry, and cultural knick-knacks, and returned to the street. The song continued to develop.

Ron with Sierra Leonean street vendors. Photo by Lenny Spears.

By the time our group returned to Cape Sierra Hotel for lunch, I shared the completed lyrics with Thomalind and Antawn and "Priscilla's Homecoming" coordinators Joseph Opala and Jacque Metz.

That evening we gathered at the U.S. Embassy, completing a full day with a lecture about "Priscilla's Homecoming" by Opala. Before beginning his talk, he asked that I share the new song with the group. I had not yet committed the words to memory but, confident the tune was fairly well etched in my mind, I consented.

I did not observe the audience of about 100 as I sang. My eyes were glued to the lyrics in my notebook. Afterwards, I was thrilled to be told that when the song concluded there was not a dry eye in the room!

Mrs. Polite said the song gave her the first glimpse of the significance of her journey. She had known she was coming, she said, and a celebration had been planned, that she was representing her family, but not until that moment did the event become *something so real, something so true.*

Teary-eyed, Thomalind Polite addressed the audience at the conclusion of an emotionally packed program, which included haunting and joyous songs of welcome by the Freetown Players, Sierra Leone's cultural ambassadors. "I wish that my father who started this could have been here with me," she said between sobs. "But I am proud to represent him and represent my family and represent Priscilla!"

"Something So Real!"

Roped as a captive…
Snatched by surprise…
Stolen from her family…
With tears in her eyes
Was a little girl—
Bound for an unknown world.

Who would be her mother now?
Who would lead and guide
This child's dreams, hopes, plans?
Would they all subside?
No, they would not die!
Through cen'tries, they would thrive!

Art by Dana Coleman. Poster design by Ideas4
and the USF Africana Heritage Project.
Courtesy, Toni Carrier, Joyce Reese McCollum, and
Africana Heritage Project, www.africanaheritage.com.

CHORUS:
Something so real! Something so true!
The past has become clear; the old now is new.
Connections bring healing. The bond is renewed.
Priscilla has come home! Her legacy endures!

Made to work the fields of rice,
Cotton and indigo,
Thousands from Sierra Leone
To America did go—
Never to return.
But now one has returned.

CHORUS:
Something so real! Something so true!
The past has become clear; the old now is new.
Connections bring healing. The bond is renewed.
Priscilla has come home! Her legacy endures!

BRIDGE:
This is not a fairy tale. No-no!
The African spirit of hope and family—anh-hanh—has prevailed!

CHORUS:
Something so real! Something so true!
The past has become clear; the old now is new.
Connections bring healing. The bond is renewed.
Priscilla has come home! Her legacy endures!
Priscilla has come home!
Her legacy—through Thomalind Martin Polite—endures!

Words and Music by Ronald Daise
© 2005

Thomalind and Antawn Polite respond with emotion as Joseph Opala tells them about the Bunce Island slave castle, from which Priscilla may have departed her homeland. Ron (in background) listens attentively.
Courtesy, Jacque Metz.

The way I useta walk, A dohn walk no mo.

There has been a great change within me since my visit to Sierra Leone. As I had felt the summer before when I visited Ghana, my experiences left me with the undeniable perception that I had traveled back home, to a place (even though I had never visited physically) I recognized—intuitively, culturally, and spiritually. On day two, I received a new name: *Kemeforay.*

The naming ceremony, officiated by Susu community male elders wearing long white, sky blue, and salmon-colored kaftans, was held at a site overlooking the Atlantic Ocean, adjacent to Cape Sierra Hotel. The female elders, regal and radiant in brightly colored dresses with complimentary head wraps, sat or stood beside them, facing the audience, at a long table draped with white cloth.

Village elders at Susu Naming Ceremony for Priscilla's Homecoming participants. Photo by author.

It was a peaceful afternoon. African rhythms by drummers and balanji players pulsated playfully, skillfully, invoking heads to nod, shoulders to sway, feet to glide. As everyone gathered, gentle breezes rustled tree leaves, and I led onlookers in "The Electric Slide"—to the enchantment of the Africans who watched the dance and soon joined in.

Cape Sierra is one of Africa's westernmost points—the point closest to South America—and is near the entrance to the great harbor, where the Bunce Island slave castle stood. "Standing here," Joseph Opala addressed those gathered for the ceremony, "it would have been possible to see the *Hare* on April 9, 1756, as it set its sails westward. It is fitting that when Priscilla's descendant returns, she should recover her African identity right here at this spot."

Thomalind received the name *N'mah Koya*, which means "great mother";

Antawn, *Dala Modu*, meaning "great warrior. My new name, *Kemeforay*, means "old man," which is a mark of respect in Sierra Leonean culture. An old man is regarded as an elder, an advisor. The Susu ruled one of the oldest and most distinguished empires of the region. Susus are Muslim. The advice of one named Kemeforay is the last secured before action is taken to resolve a family or military matter.

Ron, after having been given the Susu name Kemeforay. Photo by Lenny Spears.

The resilience, courage, and fortitude of Priscilla, has reinforced my need to promote, or, rather, *advise*, about the connections of those of West African heritage. Her life has inspired and will continue to inspire many.

On May 30, 2005, Sierra Leonean president Dr. Ahmad Tejah Kabbah, seated on a golden throne at his Hill Station office in

Ron during the Susu naming ceremony. Courtesy, Jacque Metz.

116

Manilius Garber, chairman of the Monuments and Relics Commission, receives painting of Priscilla by Dana Coleman, presented by Thomalind Martin Polite to the Sierra Leone National Museum.
Courtesy, Toni Carrier, Joyce Reese McCollum, and Africana Heritage Project, www.africanaheritage.com.

Freetown, addressed Thomalind and Antawn. "Your great-grandmother was a compatriot of mine, but somehow she found herself away from home and traveled to a place that she didn't know, under some pressure. Your great-grandmother was indeed a very visionary person to make sure that some of those records about her condition were saved, were maintained."

At a reception at the Sierra Leone National Museum, curator Celia Nicol, remarked, "In Africa, it is believed that the spirit of an African who has died is not at home until it is back in African soil." Manilius Garber, chairman of the Monuments and Relics Commission, added, "I think it was divinely led that God preserved Priscilla. Many are displaced, but you have now been set free. You can say like the Negro spiritual, `Free at last. Thank God Almighty, I'm free at last.'"

Following two successful coordinations of Gullah homecomings to Sierra Leone in 1989 and 1997, Joseph Opala was implored by Sierra Leoneans to secure a *more specific* and then an *even more specific* linkage of a Gullah family with Sierra Leonean ancestry. With "Priscilla's Homecoming," Opala considered that mission fulfilled:

> While doing research for our documentary film, I found what I never expected to see—the original records of the *Hare*, the slave ship that took Priscilla to America. Sitting in the ornate reading room of the New York Historical Society I held the dispatch Cap-

tain Godfrey sent from Sierra Leone on April 8th, 1756, the day before he sailed for Charleston, and another he wrote on June 25th soon after arriving in America. Then, to my utter astonishment, I was holding the actual records of the sale of the Africans from the *Hare*. Running my eyes quickly down the list of buyers, I saw it: "Elias/St. John's/Ball—3 boys—2 girls." There was Priscilla: one of the two little girls.

But the *Hare's* records held yet another surprise—the ship's homeport. Edward Ball had concluded that the *Hare* was a British ship owned by Bunce Island, but the records showed that while the *Hare* stopped at Bunce Island and conducted some of its business there, it was actually a Rhode Island vessel owned by Samuel and William Vernon, wealthy merchants in Newport. The foremost center in North America for ships engaged in the Atlantic slave trade, Newport sent nearly 1,000 voyages to Africa and exiled almost 100,000 people to bondage in the West Indies and the Southern Colonies.

View at Cape Sierra, from which bystanders could have seen the slave ship Hare sailing westward from Bunce Island with ten-year-old Priscilla as a captive on April 9, 1756. Photo by author.

I knew that some Rhode Island community leaders had been trying to tell the story of the Newport slave trade for years, but were meeting resistance. I was sure that the story of Priscilla—the story of just one little girl exiled by a Newport ship—would be the best way to get the message across, and so I shared my findings. Community leaders soon established "Project Priscilla" with the goal of raising one dollar each from 10,000 Rhode Islanders to send Thomalind Martin Polite to Sierra Leone and then bring her up to their state after she returns. Project Priscilla aims at joining together all three communities—Rhode Island, Sierra Leone, and South Carolina—in an "act of remembrance."

[With] Thomalind going to Sierra Leone this year, and then later to Rhode Island, I think my work finally will be done. After all, I don't see how it can get more *specific* than this. (www.yale.edu/glc/priscilla/opala.htm)

Reflections of another Priscilla's Posse member, Jeanine "Nina" Talley of Oakland, California—self-defined singer, songwriter, and author of an upcoming novel based on her travels to Sierra Leone—echoed these life-changing sentiments:

I resonated with Priscilla's story.

Priscilla's Homecoming gave me an amazing introduction to the country and history of Sierra Leone. Being in the country and having a chance to interact with the people in such an intimate and meaningful way was a blessing, in the highest form of the word.

My mind has been opened to the realities of West Africa and also to the beautiful depth and creativity of the history of its peoples. As an African American, I felt for the first time like I reconnected with the culture of my ancestors lost so long ago. That history, that shared story, has somehow reconnected me to the continent as a whole, and a sense of solidarity has been deepened with its diverse people. Of course, the opportunity to travel to Sierra Leone also presented me with my future as well as my past, as I am now [married] to a man I met after the Homecoming was over.

I have so many great memories of the week! No doubt, the most profound was walking on Bunce Island. Even though I already knew the story of the Island, being there changed everything in a way that I can't really explain through words. It's something you just have to experience for yourself. I also remember dancing "The Electric Slide" with Ron, Thomalind, and Antawn to African drums during the Susu Naming Ceremony. It was like the combination of American and African cultures melting together in a way that was really great fun!

I least expected to learn that as an African American I am part of a group of people that has two distinct and valuable histories, one European and one African, neither beginning in the Americas but having stories that go both ways for generations. Up until this point in my life I had only been aware of the first history and at times was told that that was the only one that was important. But touching the African continent and learning Priscilla's story was like listening to my own family's story, and I finally felt like I reconnected with long lost relatives. I have such gratitude for the welcome and friendliness I felt while in that country and look forward to returning home again, soon.

There aren't many people who can say that they met national dignitaries, dined with journalists, and danced the Electric Slide to African drums on their first trip to the African continent. But I can say now that I have. And for that I will always be grateful.

Upon the request of President Kabbah, Priscilla's Posse members received printed invitations to a state house dinner at 8:00 PM on Tuesday, May 31st, 2005. Noting that the attire was "Formal/National," I was elated to have packed a Kente-cloth bowtie and cummerbund I had purchased in Ghana the summer before.

Seated in the banquet hall, as waiters greeted us and poured water and wine, I was asked to share a brief Gullah presentation. The words and tune of an old Gullah/Geechee spiritual—"Great Change Since I Been Born"—invaded my thoughts. I began scratching notes onto my notepad amidst the banter of arriving guests, altering the old lyrics here and there to convey the sentiments of Priscilla's Homecoming constituents. Using Gullah and Krio words and expressions, I stood before the listening crowd and offered "We Gone Home When We Gone Salone."

The Minister of Tourism & Culture
Dr. Chernor A. Jalloh
request the company of

Roni DAISE
....

To the Official Dinner in honour of Priscilla's
Homecoming from Charleston, U.S.A. to Sierra Leone

at the Banquet Hall of State House,
State Avenue, Tower Hill, Freetown

On Tuesday, 31ˢᵗ May, 2005
At 8:00p.m.

Dress   R.S.V.P.
Formal / National   235428/242151
                          076604106/076617125

Invitation to a state house dinner in Freetown, Sierra Leone, in honor of Priscilla's Homecoming, at which Ron sang "We Gone Home When We Gone Salone."

Antawn and Thomalind Polite, Ron, and Jeanine Talley dancing "The Electric Slide" in Sierra Leone.

Sierra Leonean (left) watches the dancing with interest.
Courtesy, Alison Sutherland.

Sierra Leonean (left) joyfully joins the line dance.
Courtesy, Alison Sutherland.

"We Gone Home When We Gone Salone"

(Sung to the tune of Gullah spiritual "Great Change Since I Been Born")

We glad tummoch we gone Sierra Leone
We glad tummoch we gone Sierra Leone
We glad tummoch we gone Sierra Leone
We gone home when we gone Salone

Dey mek we crack we teet when we gone Salone
Dey mek we crack we teet—hah, hah—when we gone Salone
Dey mek we crack we teet—fa true!—when we gone Salone
We gone home when we gone Salone

We done bring Priscilla home when we gone Salone
We done bring Priscilla sperit home when we gone Salone
We done bring Priscilla way back home when we gone Salone
We gone home when we gone Salone

Salone! Salone! We hona oona, Salone!
Salone! Salone! We hona oona, Salone!
Salone! Salone! Salone! We hona oona, Salone!
We gone home when we gone Salone!

We gladi we fa gone Sierra Leone
We gladi we fa gone Sierra Leone
We beaucoup gladi we fa gone Sierra Leone
We gone home when we gone Salone
We gone home when we gone Salone
     Thomalind and Antawn
We gone home when we gone Salone
     Joseph Opala
We gone home when we gone Salone
     Rhode Island
We gone home when we gone Salone
     Sout Calina
We gone home when we gone Salone
     Georgia, too
We gone home when we gone Salone
Black and White Americans

We gone home when we gone Salone
     De Gullah People dem
We gone home when we gone Salone

Words by Ronald Daise
© 2005

"Great Change Since I Been Born"

(Gullah spiritual)

There's a great change since I been born
There's a great change since I been born
There's a great change since I been born
There's a great change since I been born

The way I used to walk, I don walk no mo
The way I used to walk, I don walk no mo
The way I used to walk, I don walk no mo
There's a great change since I been born

Things I used to say, I don say no mo
Things I used to say, I don say no mo
Things I used to say, I don say no mo
There's a great change since I been born

Friends I used to have, I don have no mo
Friends I used to have, I don have no mo
Friends I used to have, I don have no mo
There's a great change since I been born

Great change, great change since I been born
Great change, great change since I been born
Great change, great change since I been born
There's a great change since I been born

There's a great change since I been born
There's a great change since I been born
There's a great change since I been born
There's a great change since I been born

I look back an' wondah how I got ovah.

I thought about Priscilla on January 28, 2006, when I performed "Priscilla's Posse: A Press Conference about Gullah Heritage" at Fort Moultrie on Sullivan's Island, South Carolina. I pondered her stamina in surviving the perilous trans-atlantic journey at age ten and then being placed on an auction block.

> Before being placed on the auction block and sold to the highest bidder, Africans were stripped naked, washed, shaved, and rubbed with palm oil. Wounds or scars on their bodies were filled with tar. Before making purchases, potential buyers inspected the teeth and bodies of enslaved men and women in minute detail. ("Lowcountry Gullah Culture Special Resource Study, Public Draft," 20-21)

In the audience that day for the 75-minute interactive presentation of reminiscences of "Priscilla's Homecoming" were Thomalind Martin Polite (whom I was seeing for the first time following our return to the States), her two children, and her two aunts (sisters of her deceased father, Thomas Martin).

Priscilla and other enslaved Africans who were brought to South Carolina and Georgia experienced life on rice plantations, which you can read about and reflect upon as you walk "The Lowcountry Trail"—the pathway connecting past and present—at Brookgreen Gardens in Murrell's Inlet. Larger-than-lifesize sculptures by Babette Bloch depict the plantation owner, the overseer, an enslaved male African, and an enslaved female African who worked together, under the same sun, to produce the cash crop, Carolina Gold. (Daise 2006)

Africans living on Brookgreen Plantation and on surrounding tidal islands patterned West African social practices. They washed, cooked, laundered, interacted with neighbors, and engaged in storytelling among family and friends in the yards, on the steps, and under trees in slave villages. As they had done in their homelands, they used the one-roomed village cabins primarily for sleeping. Beliefs in evil spirits, such as hags, haints, and plat-eyes, were rooted in West African lore and passed along to Gullah descendants.

As a means of erasing personal identity, plantation owners called captive Africans "slaves" and *owned* them as property. Like cattle, they could be bought or sold at will. In general, rice planters were more humanitarian than the owners of cotton, indigo, or tobacco plantations, who utilized "gang labor." Under gang labor, enslaved Africans worked from sunup to sundown. To the contrary, rice plantations operated the "task system." Each enslaved worker was given a specific and difficult daily task designed to take about ten hours to complete. Used as an incentive, the task system allowed enslaved laborers who completed their work to use their time to grow their own food or tend to personal needs.

The overseer maintained a journal, or notebook, of each enslaved worker's tasks in order to manage the day-to-day operation of the plantation. A driver, usually an African, enforced the rules. Unlike elsewhere in North America, in the South, Africans were used as overseers on some rice plantations because many whites did not live year-round in the oppressively hot, mosquito-infested swampland that was similar to African environs.

According to historian Joseph Opala:

> To manage the complex work of a rice plantation and carry out the task system, low country planters placed their trust in a special individual found only in that region—the rice driver. The driver was a trusted slave—often an elderly man—who was an expert at rice farming. When the owner was away during the rainy spring and summer months, the driver was often in charge. He was the farm manager in fact, if not in name.
>
> The planters tried to select as drivers men who had an air of authority about them, men who were obviously important among the slaves themselves, or even among their own people where they came from in Africa. They wanted drivers the other slaves would look up to. It was sometimes said that plantation owners chose drivers from "African royalty."
>
> The drivers often assigned the farm tasks and decided on punishments. White overseers had to get along with the experi-

enced drivers. They were like a 2nd lieutenant who has to get along with his older and more experienced sergeant. Slave though he was, the driver was important, and without him nothing got done on the plantation.

I have seen a letter Henry Laurens wrote to the overseer of one of his rice plantations in the late 1700s. Laurens fired the white man because he couldn't get along with Old Cuffy, the driver. Laurens told his overseer that if he couldn't get along with Cuffy, then he was useless to him on the plantation. He fired the white man and told him to give the keys to the plantation buildings to Cuffy and come to Charleston to collect his pay.

There are some well-known cases of drivers who were devout Muslims and who arrived from Africa already able to read and write in Arabic. Later in the 19th century, after the trans-Atlantic slave trade was outlawed, some drivers were literate in English. They sent letters during the summer months to the plantation owners who had taken refuge outside the mosquito-ridden low country, explaining how things were going on the farm during the owner's absence." (Personal communication, Joseph Opala, May 11, 2005)

This 1830s slave cabin located in Friendfield Village on Hobcaw Barony, Georgetown, South Carolina, like others, was used primarily for sleeping. Patterning West African social practices, enslaved Africans washed, cooked, laundered, and interacted with neighbors in the yards, on the steps, and under trees in slave villages. Courtesy, Belle W. Baruch Foundation.

On rice plantations, the rhythms hearkened back to the seasonal changes of West African rice communities—times for planting, growing, harvesting, threshing. All worked together "Unda the Same Sun" (sung to the tune of the spiritual "Feel Like Journey On").

It was easy to imagine Priscilla's thoughts as she grew accustomed to the new rhythm of life in South Carolina. She found herself working on a plantation—enslaved, no longer with an opportunity of developing into a free woman—working on land the Elders around her did *not* own and doing work that did *not* contribute to the well being of her community of workers.

She found herself struggling to bond with others who may have looked familiar but who were *not* her relatives.

And she found herself watching the seasons change. . . . year after year . . . and to an order that was *not* as she had witnessed during her first ten years of life. This order was new . . . and harsh . . . and different.

At times I have wondered how Priscilla and other enslaved Africans came to grips with changes in time-honored customs and traditions like burial practices, and having to adapt to new ones like Watch Night services.

Africans brought to America a world view and burial practices which were quite different from those of Europeans. Although Africa is composed of many cultures and ethnic groups, some basic characteristics are shared by all. The cosmos is divided into two realms, the visible and invisible worlds. The visible world consists of all things and people presently found on Earth. The invisible world, with the supreme being at the top, is populated by many beings, including spirits of the recently deceased and nature spirits. The deceased, known as "the living dead," continue to exist in the invisible world as spirits.

The family may communicate with the deceased in visions and dreams and may ask for assistance from the spirit. Graves are used as a way of communicating with the dead. They are decorated with household items and the possessions of the deceased in an attempt to satisfy the needs of the spirit, which occupies the watery world of the dead. Grave decorations symbolize the spiritual world by the artifacts placed on the graves. Black burial practices and mortuary goods have been extensively studied by ethnographers and folklorists, who have established that household items, placed on the African-American grave represent the continuation of West African traditions and beliefs about the spirit world.

Plants and trees also symbolize the life of the spirit. The roots of the tree grow downward into the spirit world, while the tree symbolizes the living spirit. In the Congo today, trees are planted on the grave because, in the words of one elder, "The tree is a sign of the spirit on its way to another world." During the 1930s a popular custom among Blacks was placing evergreens on the grave as part of the funeral ceremony. If the tree survived, this was taken as a sign that "all was well with the soul." (Nichols, 52)

And if having to make adaptations to everyday customs did not confound them, how did the newly transported Africans maintain the resilience to start new traditions like Watch Night services? They used such events to look back and wonder how they got over—year after year. The practice energized them.

Watch Night Services initially were held in the plantation prayer houses. Beginning at 10 p.m. on New Year's Eve, Islanders assembled to sing rousing spirituals, pray and testify until five minutes before midnight. Doing the Shout would highlight the ceremony.

The Shout was not a vocal response, but a way of praising the Lord with the feet. Everyone would do the Shout, glorifying God for what He had done for them during the year. People would encircle the room, singing a spiritual until they had set the song. Then the beat would quicken. An excitement, a spiritual fervor would begin to move within their bodies. The people clapped their hands. Soon, their praises migrated to their feet. They would Shout!

The Shout was like doing the Charleston [the dance]. But the feet were never crossed, which would signify worldly dancing. Instead, they were moved sprightly to either side. . . . With their singing, testifying, and praising, the Islanders rejoice until five minutes before midnight. Then all the lights in the church building are turned off. The congregation kneels in silent prayer.

Four men called "travelers" assemble in each corner of the building. Alternately, each "traveler" sings this request to a leader at the front of the room: "Watchman, watchman, tell me the hour of the night."

The "watchman," in turn, states the time in song, concluding that all is well. At midnight, he proclaims, "Traveler, traveler, traveler—it is twelve o'clock, and all is well. HAPPY NEW YEAR!"

As members rise to their feet, the lights are turned on. Eyes are alight with reverence as the Islanders reflect on God's goodness throughout the past year. Their eyes, too, are aglow with marvel as they greet neighbors and friends. For they have come this far. They will journey on." (Daise 1986, 101–102)

As I performed at Fort Moultrie, I imagined Priscilla watching the seasons change to a familiar rhythm that was etched on her DNA—the rhythm of planting, growing, harvesting, threshing. This rhythm pulsed without interruption as she lived among and worked for others who were different than her African self . . . who also toiled "Unda the Same Sun."

Sullivan's Island was a quarantine station where pest houses were located. The pest houses were built to contain all persons with contagious diseases before they entered the port of Charleston: domestic travelers, persons from the Mediterranean, as well as enslaved Africans. Tens of thousands of captives from West African shores first touched soil in North America there between 1700 and 1775 before impacting the American mosaic. Courtesy, National Park Service.

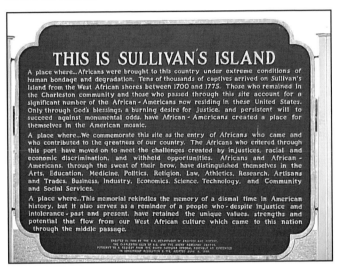

THIS IS SULLIVAN'S ISLAND

A place where ... Africans were brought to this country under extreme conditions of human bondage and degradation. Tens of thousands of captives arrived on Sullivan's Island from the West African shores between 1700 and 1775. Those who remained in the Charleston community and those who passed through this site account for a significant number of the African-Americans now residing in these United States. Only through God's blessings, a burning desire for justice, and persistent will to succeed against monumental odds, have African-Americans created a place for themselves in the American mosaic.

A place where ... We commemorate this site as the entry of Africans who came and who contributed to the greatness of our country. The Africans who entered through this port have moved on to meet the challenges created by injustices, racial and economic discrimination, and withheld opportunities. Africans and African-Americans, through the sweat of their brow, have distinguished themselves in the Arts, Education, Medicine, Politics, Religion, Law, Athletics, Research, Artisans and Trades, Business, Industry, Economics, Science, Technology, and Community and Social Services.

A place where ... This memorial rekindles the memory of a dismal time in American history, but it also serves as a reminder of a people who—despite injustice and intolerance—past and present, have retained the unique values, strengths and potential that flow from our West African culture which came to this nation through the middle passage.

"Unda the Same Sun"

(Sung to the tune of Gullah spiritual "Feel Like Journey On")

Unda the same sun/and with one vision
    They grew Carolina Gold
All toiled together on the rice plantations
    They grew Carolina Gold

Europeans sold land to Americans
    They grew Carolina Gold
To work the fields of rice, they enslaved Africans
    They grew Carolina Gold

There was the Planter, there was the Overseer
    They grew Carolina Gold
There were the Africans snatched from their homelands dear
    They grew Carolina Gold

Unda the same sun/and with one vision
    They grew Carolina Gold
All toiled together on the rice plantations
    They grew Carolina Gold

Some grew rich, some died from the strain
    They grew Carolina Gold
The African's skill and strength brought others financial gain
    They grew Carolina Gold

Unda the same sun/and with one vision
    They grew Carolina Gold
All toiled together on the rice plantations
    They grew Carolina Gold

CHORUS: (HUM)

Words by Ronald Daise
© 2005

Plantation Owner   Overseer

Courtesy, Brookgreen Gardens, Murrell's Inlet, South Carolina, a National Historic Landmark. Photos by author.

Enslaved African Male   Enslaved African Female

Courtesy, Babette Bloch.

Artist Babette Bloch said of the sculptures she created for The Lowcountry Trail at Brookgreen Gardens: "These sculptures were placed here so that we could understand our past and embrace our future. They are portals of time gone by, mirrors to our souls. I believe these sculptures will evoke a range of emotions from pride of place to mourning. They are echoes of the lives that lived on this historic site."

"Feel Like Journey On"

(Gullah spiritual, from *Reminiscences of Sea Island Heritage*)

Well, I come this far, fin' no fault, feel like journey on.
Come this far, fin' no fault, feel like journey on.

If religion wuz a thing that money could buy —
    Feel like journey on.
The rich would live an' the po' would die!
    Feel like journey on.

Well, I come this far, fin' no fault, feel like journey on.
Come this far, fin' no fault, feel like journey on.

The Jerden Rivah is chilly an' col' —
    Feel like journey on.
It chills my body but not my soul.
    Feel like journey on.

Well, I come this far, fin' no fault, feel like journey on.
Come this far, fin' no fault, feel like journey on.

Upon the mountain, my God spoke —
    Feel like journey on.
Out of His mouth came fire an' smoke!
    Feel like journey on.

Well, I come this far, fin' no fault, feel like journey on.
Come this far, fin' no fault, feel like journey on.

"How I Got Ovah"

(Gullah spiritual, from *Reminiscences of Sea Island Heritage*)

How I got ovah.
How I got ovah.
I look back an' wondah how I got ovah.

Went down to the valley one day to pray.
        I look back an' wondah how I got ovah.
My soul got happy an' I stayed all day!
        I look back an' wondah how I got ovah.

I prayed an' got ovah.
I prayed an' got ovah.
I look back an' wondah how I got ovah.

I nevah been ta Heaven but I been tol' —
        I look back an' wondah how I got ovah.
The streets up there are pave' with gol'.
        I look back an' wondah how I got ovah.

I sang an' got ovah.
I sang an' got ovah.
I look back an' wondah how I got ovah.

If you get there befo'e I do —
        I look back an' wondah how I got ovah.
Tell all my friends I'm comin', too!
        I look back an' wondah how I got ovah.

My God brought me ovah!
My God brought me ovah!
I look back an' wondah how I got ovah!

I'd hear the music, then start to dance.
Africans would look at me and say, "A undastan..."
There's a connection deep down in my spirit
With Africa. West Africa.

"Nshira Nka Mikra"
("My Soul Been Bless")

My feet done touch de soil een Africa, een Ghana, Sweet Moda
    Africa
My feet done touch de soil een Africa
An I been bless
My soul been bless

My soul done greet my ancestas een Africa, een
    Ghana, Sweet Moda Africa
My soul done
    greet my
    ancestas een
    Africa
An I been bless
My soul been
    bless

Photos courtesy, Don Clerico,
Charleston Southern University.

RAP:
Ebryboddy stoop an carry bundles on dey head
Fish, wata, eggs, wood, grounduts an bread
Dey neva stoop een dey spirit, dough,
Dey proud, dey free
Dey walk tall, proud, wit dignity

My ears done heah de drumbeat een Africa, een Ghana, Sweet
    Moda Africa
My ears done heah de drumbeat een Africa
An I been bless. My soul been bless

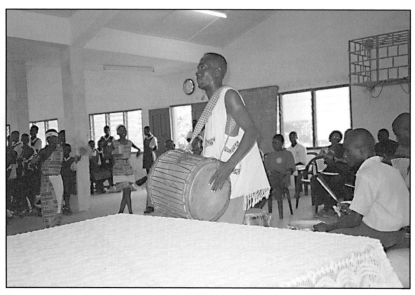

Photos courtesy, Don Clerico, Charleston Southern University.

My eyes done see majesty in Africa, een Ghana, Sweet Moda
    Africa
My eyes done see majesty een Africa
An I been bless. My soul been bless

RAP:
"Welcome home!" ancient voices call softly
De echo swell gran and tall like de keypok tree
People's eyes, noses, heads look like my family's
An een de ebenin dakness gently falls black like me

Courtesy, Don Clerico, Charleston Southern University.

I feel de breat ob Mighty Gawd een Africa, in Ghana, Sweet Moda
    Africa
I feel de breat ob Mighty Gawd een Africa
An I been bless. My soul been bless

Courtesy, Don Clerico,
Charleston Southern University.

Photo by author.

Courtesy, Don Clerico,
Charleston Southern University.

Photo by author.

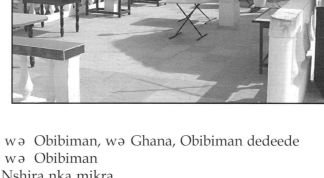

Mi nan aka asaase wə Obibiman, wə Ghana, Obibiman dedeede
Mi nan aka asaase wə Obibiman
Na manya nshira. Nshira nka mikra
Na manya nshira. Nshira nka mikra
An I been bless. My soul been bless.

Words and Music by Ronald Daise
Musical Arrangement by Vernon B. Harris
© 2004

In slave castles, I'd hear the groans
Of ancestors moaning, "We are one!"
There's a connection deep down in my spirit
With Africa. West Africa.

"African Diaspora"

Diaspora, Diaspora, Diaspora, Diaspora . . .
African Diaspora
set the seeds afloat.
Diaspora.
The seeds and the spores
went to unknown shores,
scattered throughout Diaspora.
Diaspora . . . Diaspora . . .
African Diaspora.

Huddled in the ships of the Middle Passage
Shackled and chained and whipped with lashes,
Some Africans endured, others fought,
some jumped overboard, with this one thought:
"Oh, freedom, oh, freedom
Oh, freedom ova me
An befo I be a slave
I be bury in my grave
An go home to my Lawd an be free!"

Diaspora, Diaspora, Diaspora, Diaspora . . .
African Diaspora
set the seeds afloat.
Diaspora.
The seeds and the spores
went to unknown shores,
scattered throughout Diaspora.
Diaspora . . . Diaspora . . .
African Diaspora.

"Signs, Stories, Solutions"

The SIGNS
at Cape Coast Castle
and
Elmina Castle
dungeons and bastions of slavery and colonialism
which overlook the Atlantic Ocean
in Ghana, West Africa
made me
contort within
made me
scream
weep
bristle
gasp
wretch
writhe

Photos courtesy, Don Clerico, Charleston Southern University.

144

SIGN — "MEN'S DUNGEON"
dark
dank
dreary with lingering despair
of bodies, huddled and fearful
eyes, searching for sunlight
ears, listening for familiar voices or moans of
Mother, Father, Sister, Wife, Daughter, Brother, Son
lungs, bursting for air to keep breathing
keep hoping
keep living

SIGN — "FEMALE DUNGEONS" and "FEMALE SLAVE YARD"
horrendous
horrifying
hostile—even though centuries have passed
harbors without dignity or refuge for the countless lives
that nobly birthed nations
courageously scratched and bit and butted
governors and soldiers
who disgraced their flesh and their spirits
even while chains harnessed their ankles

SIGN — "CELLS"
ghastly
ghostly
grave of blood stains
and bones mashed into mortar
and heard-but-not-cared-about anguished screams
garrison where "hostile captives"
were placed together in a
solitary

CELL
without ventilation
with sometimes up to 150 others
until the last survivor
breathed his last breath
a mass burial followed
before THE CELL
began to collect
new captives
who fought back
who
wanted
to be free

Photos courtesy, Don Clerico, Charleston Southern University.

SIGN — "CELL"
(doorway framed with skull and crossed sword blades)
here
the guards who helped the Africans
or showed them any act of kindness
were shoved
storaged
starved

SIGN — "GOVERNOR'S BEDROOM AND OFFICES"
upstairs
spacious
serenely
overlooking the tranquility of the Atlantic Ocean
as well as
the anything-but-serene madness
on
The Block
below
where Africans
were traded
sold
torn
from their homeland
ripped away from
freedom
because of someone's love of
sugar
money
power
rum

Photos courtesy, Don Clerico, Charleston Southern University.

SIGN—"CHURCH"
can you
believe
the
incongruity . . .
a
center of worship
praising the God of Life
erected
at the center
of
hell on earth
where disregard of life, love, and human kindness
was championed:
a conundrum beyond belief

SIGN — "DOOR OF NO RETURN"
once passed
the Middle Passage was begun
and
"hope"
"heritage"
"home"
took on new meaning
and
the confusion and struggle for comprehension
continue
to this day

Photos courtesy, Don Clerico, Charleston Southern University.

The SIGNS
at Cape Coast Castle
and
Elmina Castle
dungeons and bastions of slavery and colonialism
which overlook the Atlantic Ocean
in Ghana, West Africa
should not be forgotten
or allowed to decay
so that when others see them
and also
contort within
scream
weep
bristle
gasp
wretch
writhe
then
such reminders of such gross inhumanity
will never again
need to become
SIGNS

Courtesy, Don Clerico, Charleston Southern University.

Soon one morning,
Death come creepin een ma room.

When I recall my visit to Bunce Island and consider the atrocities that prevailed there, I'm disturbed at a cellular level. I inhale slowly, deeply and exhale a cleansing breath to release feelings of funereal gloom. Bunce Island houses the ruins of the slave castle in the Sierra Leone River. Africans brought there had been marched from the interior by warring African tribes who sold them as slaves to Europeans for cloth, alcohol, metal goods, guns, and trinkets. Known for its elegant Great House, or headquarters building, where the English traders held lavish dinners, Bunce Island is an important historical relic, which, for me, evoked sentiments of tears, struggle, death. The dining area overlooks the prison, or open slave yard, immediately to the rear of the Great House. The island has been uninhabited since 1840.

Africans were brought to the upriver side of Bunce Island in small boats — chained together, single file. They were examined like animals. Their teeth, eyes, ears, and genitals were examined with scrutiny. Like cattle, they were branded on their shoulder — with RACE for Royal African Company of England. They were made to eat from troughs, while they were chained together, in the open, in separate male and female slave yards — until they were marched to the slave ships on the downriver side of the castle. They feared they would be cooked or boiled and eaten.

Historian Joseph Opala told participants in Priscilla's Homecoming about the Bunce Island "warehouse of humanity" during filming of a documentary about the event. As I absorbed details and facts, I saw and touched centuries-old cannons and meandered in and out of door openings to the male and female slave yards. Feelings of unbelief, fear, and horror still permeate the Bunce Island environs.

Escaping was highly improbable, Opala told us, because Bunce Island was a double-door prison, surrounded by man-eating crocodiles. Not long before our visit, he said, diggers at an area near the slave yards had discovered the jaw of a child. Children brought to Bunce Island and boarded upon slave ships often died during the Middle Passage (the name given to the transatlantic crossing to the New World, the middle leg of the slave journey). Caleb Godfrey, captain of the *Hare*, set sail from Sierra Leone in April 1756 with eighty-four enslaved Africans. Sixteen died on the ten-week voyage to Charleston. Priscilla and four other children were sold to Elias Ball. Priscilla may have been brought to Bunce Island—more likely, she had been made to remain aboard the ship, *Hare*, as it sat in the harbor near the island, waiting for other captives to be brought aboard.

About one of every twenty Africans taken across the Atlantic went to North America, while nineteen of every twenty were carried to the West Indies and Brazil. During the era of slave trade, about forty-three percent of Africans taken to South Carolina came from the Rice Coast of West Africa, including Sierra Leone.

Thomas N. Hull, United States Ambassador to Sierra Leone, proclaims, "Bunce Island is one of my favorite places. It's really stunning! Whatever your

Antawn and Thomalind Polite sit in contemplation with Joseph Opala in front of the castle and prison ruins at Bunce Island. Photo by author.

ethnic heritage, when you get there, the tragedy and the immensity of the slave trade just hits you—the cruelty of it. It's there when you visualize, and you can readily visualize—despite the fact that it's ruins—what went on there, how people were brought down to the island and then shipped off."

Antawn Polite witnessed Hull's proclamation firsthand and said he had to still himself during the Bunce Island tour because it made him sick and sad. "It looks like a beautiful island when you see it," he said. "It doesn't hit you until you hit the island and learn the history. To the untrained eye, anybody who sees it would think, `Oh, what a beautiful island!' and think it's a vacation spot. But when you realize how isolated it is, you know why [you feel that way]. And I really feel the way the Africans felt. And being an African-American, it brings back a lot of memories—that my ancestors were branded like cattle and that even though they took measures to try to make things better, it still is pretty hard to swallow." (Frazier. Interview with Antawn Polite at Bunce Island.)

The Bunce Island Preservation Initiative (BIPI) Sierra Leone was established in 2005 with the understanding that "these remnants are endowed with a deep-rooted historical and spiritual significance to African-Americans and Sierra Leoneans alike that must be preserved for present and future generations. Its preservation and promotion will educate people throughout the world about the Atlantic slave trade and its terrible cost in wasted lives and broken families." (BIPI brochure)

"It's a bridge between the peoples of our two countries," Hull said. "Even though it's a bridge under tragic circumstances, it is, nevertheless, a connection to the United States, which this entire visit represents."

My feelings echo the sentiments expressed in the BIPI brochure. Bunce Island is indeed endowed with an unsettling significance that leaves visitors experiencing "tears an horra."

Thomalind and Antawn Polite listen to Joseph Opala at the Bunce Island slave castle ruins.
Courtesy, Leslie Anderson Morales.

156

"Tears an Horra"

(Sung to the tune of Gullah spiritual "Trouble Will Be Ova")

Tears an horra at Bunce Islan…
Tears an horra at Bunce Islan…
Africans on slave ships last saw their homeland
When they left from Bunce Islan

In a deep wide harbor near Sierra Leone,
There was once a castle that was well-known
Africans on slave ships last saw their homeland
When they left from Bunce Islan

Africans were brought from far and near
To this slave-trade prison they all feared
Africans on slave ships last saw their homeland
When they left from Bunce Islan

The British built this castle; it once was grand
But now its ruins are all that stand
Africans on slave ships last saw their homeland
When they left from Bunce Islan

The startling ruins of the double-door Bunce Island castle show
remnants on the male and female slave yards. Courtesy, Alison Sutherland.

Time ticks, and the ruins fade away….
Haunting memories forever stay
Ee-ee-ee-ee-ee — o-o-o-o-o
Uu-uu-uu-uu-uu-uu — aa-aa

The ancestors' heartaches prevail
In the winds their voices wail,
(SPOKEN) "Dey march us out to de slave ships. We last see ouah
    homeland
When we lef from Bunce Islan"

Tears an horra at Bunce Islan…
Tears an horra at Bunce Islan…
Africans on slave ships last saw their homeland
When they left from Bunce Islan

Aa-aa-aa-aa-aa-aa — uu-uu
Uu-uu-uu-uu-uu-uu — aa-aa
Ee-ee-ee-ee-ee — o-o-o-o-o
Uu-uu-uu-uu-uu-uu — aa-aa

Words by Ronald Daise
© 2005

A line of cannons, each bearing the monogrammed insignia of the King of England, point downriver in front of the Bunce Island castle ruins. Courtesy, Toni Carrier, Joyce Reese McCollum, and Africana Heritage Project, www.africanaheritage.com.

"Trouble Will Be Ovah"

(Gullah spiritual, from *Reminiscences of Sea Island Heritage*)

Trouble will be ovah. Amen.
Trouble will be ovah. Amen.
Trouble will be ovah when I see Jesus.
Trouble will be ovah. Amen.

The thunder rolling. Amen.
The thunder rolling. Amen.
The thunder rolling when I see Jesus.
Trouble will be ovah. Amen.

The lightning flashing. Amen.
The lightning flashing. Amen.
The lightning flashing when I see Jesus.
Trouble will be ovah. Amen.

I spied a lighthouse. Amen.
I spied a lighthouse. Amen.
I spied a lighthouse when I see Jesus.
Trouble will be ovah. Amen.

Trouble will be ovah. Amen.
Trouble will be ovah. Amen.
Trouble will be ovah when I see Jesus.
Trouble will be ovah. Amen.

Africa. West Africa.
Africa. West Africa.
There's a connection deep down in my spirit
With Africa. West Africa.

The Rock That Is Higher

The audience sang movingly, "Lead me to the Rock that is higher than I. Lead me. Oh, lead me. Lead me to the Rock that is higher than I. Thou has been a shelter for me."

Feet pounded the double rhythm to the old spiritual onto the wooden church floor. Hands clapped in tempo.

The leader soloed the call:

"I neba been been ta heabn bot I been tol . . ."

And the audience responded:

"Thou has been a shelter for me!"

Again, the a cappella response followed the call:

"De streets up dere are pave wit gol . . ."

"Thou has been a shelter for me!"

As the chorus swelled, the song rocked the congregation, the floors, the spirit: "Lead me to the rock that is higher than I. Lead me. Oh, lead me. Lead me to the Rock that is higher than I. Thou has been a shelter for me!"

I, Chansome Leeson, had heard and sung the song hundreds of times throughout my childhood in Jacksonville, Florida. Yet this time was markedly different. Sadness swept over me like a chilly breeze before a rainstorm. I sat motionless, in stark contrast to those around me. Men and women stood, raising hands, stomping feet, clapping hands, swaying bodies as the song fed their souls, filled them with joy.

The program at historic Brick Baptist Church on St. Helena Island, South Carolina, was part of the annual Penn Center Heritage Days festival. It was an old-fashioned praise house service to commemorate old spirituals sung by the Gullah people, descendants of West Africans brought to South Carolina and Georgia plantations.

Then a junior history major at Hampton University, I traveled to the festival upon the recommendation of the university's museum curator, Van Ward.

The festival was a yearly mecca for him, and he assured me it would be a life-changing experience.

My nerves began to tingle as the song progressed, and I began to feel unsettled.

"Some of the spirituals were used as coded message songs," the program moderator had explained earlier in the service. "When the songs included words like `heaven' or `home," he'd said, "they may have meant places of freedom like Canada or Ohio or even back to Africa."

I squirmed, restless, in the crowded pew as I continued listening to the song. My eyes darted to the left . . . to the right . . . to the front . . . then upward, toward a chandelier, and I counted twelve small, domed light bulbs.

In celebration of their heritage, many audience members, who had traveled from communities across the United States, were dressed in colorful African attire. Men sported kofis on their heads and wore colorful dashikis. Women nodded their heads to the music. Their headdresses of batik and kente matched their regal dresses and became prisms, myriad rainbows throughout the room.

I closed my eyes, beginning to lose my grip on reality. I felt as though I was having an out-of-body experience. And then . . . I saw a vision. Eerie. Surreal.

A tall, muscular African male crouched to touch his leg. Blood and pus oozed from a sore caused by the chafing of his ankle irons. His dark face contorted in pain. Then anguish. Then horror. He seemed to have seen or heard something terrifying before he stopped moving and crouched

Sweat poured down across his facial tribal marks. The whites of his eyes flittered about furtively. He looked back at the shorter, younger male chained behind him.

"Pikworo," he whispered. He looked ahead and then back to the young male, scanning the men and women, boys and girls who followed.

"Pikworo. Salaga."

His eyes looked to heaven as tears rolled down his cheeks. Walking continued. The group of thirty to forty-five trudged slowly through the African bush. They were dressed in sparse clothing and led by two gruff-looking men. Each had tribal markings unlike those of the chained individuals. The two Africans in charge carried guns, which they pointed at the group whenever movement slowed or someone stumbled or fell. They both carried flasks filled with rum.

The whisper from the first chained man passed down the line of captives.

"Pikworo. Salaga. . . . Pikworo. Salaga."

They obviously all knew the meaning. Regrettably, I did not. The head of each adult drooped in despair as the words fell on their ears. The youngsters saw the reactions, questioned the elders, then became zombie-like as they were pulled along—all eyes drained of hope and filled with alarm.

I jerked upright. The song had ended and applause reverberated throughout the building. A chill rushed through my body. The vision was gone.

I looked around the church, surveying the faces. Surely someone else had heard the voices . . . seen the vision.

Everyone looked directly ahead, however, smiling, awaiting the next spiritual or testimony or prayer. I alone seemed to have undergone the experience. Later, drained and undone, I left Brick Baptist Church with the others, all shaking hands and embracing, touched with an inner spiritual connection and enlightenment.

Throughout the night, I nursed an inner dread. Would I again hear those voices? See the vision? And the words—Pikworo, Salaga—what did they mean? Why had the Africans cried with such remorse when the words had been spoken?

The next day at the festival, I attended the symposium, "Places of Terror along the Route to the African Diapora." My heart lunged when the lecturer spoke. She spoke the strange words from my vision.

They weren't the names of the prisoners' guards. They weren't African words for wild, ferocious animals. They were places of terror in Ghana, West Africa, for Africans captured by other Africans and sold as slaves.

"Pikworo was also called `Place of the Rocks,'" explained Professor Sally Damba of the University of Cape Coast, Ghana. "Captured tribesmen and women were herded there by Samori Toure, a Mandingo, and Babato, from Mali. They were two renegade African chiefs who partnered and sold hundreds of thousands of Africans to European slave traders.

"Pikworo is a site of large boulders that to this day glisten in the African sun.

Some sit solitarily. Others lie stacked together or near each other, forming a hilly tableau before the landscape cascades to a tree strewn savanna.

"From Pikworo, the African captives walked in chains to the Salaga Slave Market where they were nailed to a large baobab tree while the Dutch and Portuguese officials bartered rum and guns to the two African chiefs for their human bounty. From Salaga, the Africans, tired and diseased, with cuts and wounds from their walking, trekked to Elmina Castle on Ghana's coast. There they were boarded onto slave ships and bound for the treacherous journey across the Middle Passage to the Caribbean Islands, Puerto Rico, Cuba, Trinidad, Brazil and North America."

I was spellbound by her words. Why had I seen the vision? What did it mean? Without thinking, I jumped to my feet.

"Ex-excuse. Ex-cuse me. Please . . ." I stammered, not yet fully conscious of my reasons for rising.

All eyes in the room turned toward me. I held my breath, then inhaled deeply.

"Um. Well, last night. . . . Last night at Brick Church, we were singing a song during the praise house service. And . . . I, uhn, I had a-a-a vision. I saw a . . . a . . . chain gang of Africans, and they spoke the words that Professor Damba has been talking about today. . . ."

A forty-something, robust-voiced, caramel-colored woman with brownish-red sisterlocks interrupted. "Speak, brother!" Her almond-shaped eyes pleaded with me to be confident and continue.

"Go ahead, Son," the lecturer encouraged from the stage.

"I'm sorry to interrupt," I continued. "But since last night . . . until you began speaking, I've been . . . unsure. Maybe someone here can help me make sense of things."

I explained the events of the vision in detail, recounting how it had begun while the audience sang "Lead Me to the Rock That Is Higher Than I" and had ended with the haunting echo of "Pikworo. Salgaga. . . . Pikworo. Salaga" just as the song stopped.

The symposium participants looked to one another, murmuring. Following a pregnant pause, Professor Damba rested her elbow on the lecture and cupped her chin with her right hand. Her index finger began slowly tapping her left cheekbone. "Ahn-hanh! . . . Ahn-hanh! . . . Ladies and gentlemen, brothers and sisters," she began, "perhaps we've received a vision from the ancestors to remind us of the pain and suffering they endured leaving Mother Africa."

"Um-hm!" a black-coffee-colored elder man pronounced. "Now we movin! Take it slow."

Some in the audience chuckled. All listened.

"Pikworo, as I told you earlier," Professor Damba continued, "was called `Place of the Rocks.' The African prisoners of war ate on the rocks, danced on the rocks, waited on the rocks, prayed to God for deliverance on the rocks, slept on the rocks.

"They danced on what was called 'Entertainment Rock,' but their dancing wasn't because of joy or merriment. . . . Whenever Africans from Pikworo village pounded different sections of Entertainment Rock, a cacophony of different sounds erupted. The effect of the pounding was contagious. Some of the shackled African prisoners, from numerous other countries, may have danced instinctively. But all were made to dance, or, rather, to move or flail their limbs as exercise for a long and arduous journey.

"Some rebelled. These were seated on and chained to a large rock—'Punishment Rock' it was called—and whipped until they died. Their bones are buried right there among the rocks.

"Others, regrettably, were chipped away from Africa's fertile soil and culture. I'm speaking to some of you who are their descendants right now."

"Nah! Nah!" interrupted a smooth-faced, middle-school-aged boy dressed in stylish ghetto-gear and sporting a close-clipped haircut. "You mean Africans sold other Africans into . . . slavery?"

"That's not right! That just can't be right," an older teen girl added. Her

Pikworo, also known as Place of the Rocks, is located in northern Ghana. Sections were named for areas where certain activities occurred: Entertainment Rock, Punishment Rock, etc. Here, Ron dances with Pikworo children to rhymic sounds made when rocks at Entertainment Rock are pounded.

long braided extensions were pulled atop her head, gathered into a scunchie, and they cascaded backward as she strained her gaze upward and shook her head in disbelief. The composure of her "do" juxtaposed the confusion and perplexity in her eyes.

"Yes," Professor Damba stated quietly, with obvious remorse. "Yes. Yes, it did happen. Pikworo villagers only opened the site to the public in the year 2000. They were ashamed of their ancestors' participation in the slave trade. Ashamed. And rightfully so. But it is a part of our country's history. . . . Perhaps if they had not participated, they would have been overtaken by other villagers who had received guns from the Europeans.

"The slave trade was an evil, evil system. Once Africans got involved in it, whether or not they knew fully, from the beginning, what they were doing, it was almost impossible to unravel their way out.

"Perhaps this young man's vision was to make us see more clearly and think more collectively. I don't know. Let's see . . . the song that somehow invoked his vision was 'Lead Me to the Rock?' Well, did most of you attend the service? Did you sing the song?"

Almost everyone raised hands. Some began softly humming the tune, but that soon faded.

"Everyone who heard it and sang it—black or white, male or female—let's pledge to lead our brothers and sisters of the African Diaspora to another rock."

Heads nodded. Feet stomped the floor in affirmation.

"A rock of love? With no suffering?" chimed in an elementary-school-aged, pecan-colored little girl two rows ahead of me. The man seated besider her—her dad, I supposed—patted her back. As she smiled and shook her head, basking in his approval, numerous braids with colorful barrettes jiggled.

"That's just what we need, little one," Professor Damba said, pointing triumphantly in the little girl's direction. "A rock of love and trust and harmony. Anh-hanh! Gullah people, Brazilian people, Caribbean people, Haitian people, African people, American people, let us lead each other to this rock. It is higher that we are. It will be a shelter for us!"

Applause filled the room, and jubilant *a cappella* voices began singing the spiritual.

Humbled and uplifted, I sat smiling.

A voice from the past had set a course for the future.

I want to climb up higher and higher, higher and higher, higher and higher.

In the Gullah folktale "The People Could Fly," which I presented in songs and narrative during my Priscilla's Homecoming performance of "Dream Weaving, Gullah Stories & Songs" at the British Council, a group of enslaved Africans sprout wings and fly away. Tired of suffering, longing for home, and unbound by fear, the characters listen to magic words called out by an old African and find themselves rising upward. Soon they are winging above and away from the plantation owner and overseer until they are *going . . . going . . . gone*. Virginia Hamilton cites the story as "a powerful testament to the millions of slaves who never had the opportunity to `fly away.' They remained slaves, as did their children. `The People Could Fly' was first told and retold by those who had only their imaginations to set them free." (Hamilton, 173)

Numerous events during Priscilla's Homecoming are testaments and reminders that people, indeed, *can* fly! Four occurred on two distinct, magical and momentous dates.

"This is a powerful story for African Americans because every African American yearns to find where they came from on this great continent," Joseph Opala said when introducing Thomalind Martin Polite to Sierra Leone president Alhaji Dr. Ahmad Tejan Kabbah. "And yet this is a very exceptional case of someone who can do that because of the accident of historical preservation. Personally, because of my long association with Sierra Leone, I could not be more delighted because, in this case, it turns out her ancestor came from here in Sierra Leone . . . and we know that all the fifty-five years that she lived as a slave, she would have dreamed of coming home everyday."

This account is, in itself, immensely uplifting! Two days later, however, my spirit buoyed even higher. Following an emotionally draining day trip to Bunce Island, where we toured the ruins of the infamous British slave castle from

Chief Alimamy Rakka of Sangbulima Village, Tasso Island, Sierra Leone, extended blessings to Antawn Polite and Thomalind Polite and their descendants during Priscilla's Homecoming. Courtesy, Jacque Metz.

which Thomalind's ancestor left Africa, we stopped at Tasso Island. Each site is accessible only by boat.

We enjoyed an interesting reception with Alimamy Rakka, chief of Sangbulima Village on Tasso Island. Some twenty years prior to our visit, Opala had met the chief and inquired about his awareness of African descendants taken across the Atlantic Ocean from the nearby slave castle. Chief Rakka had responded that his parents and grandparents told him about Sierra Leoneans captured and put on big ships, but he and his villagers had no idea what happened to them. No idea. No sense of connection.

Now, the connection had come full circle! On our visit that day, Chief Rakka, who appeared to be 95 to 100 years old, sat beside Thomalind's husband Antawn and extended blessings to him and to Thomalind and her offspring — direct descendants of an African who is believed to have left two-and-a-half centuries earlier from the nearby slave castle, and who, according to Opala, probably came from a Susu village somewhere in what is now northern Sierra Leone or neighboring Guinea.

Thomalind addressed President Kabbah. "Thank you once again," she said, "for receiving me and my family and my extended family who have come along with me to my home. When Joseph Opala and Jacqueline Metz first came to me with that letter [of invitation to travel to Sierra Leone], I did not expect to feel the way I do today. I am very proud and very honored to be able to return home and to return Priscilla home. I just know that Priscilla is at peace, that she is home after so many years, after 249 years. And I am very proud to represent her today and to show the strength, the survival that she had back in Charleston, surviving the journey and also the many years of slavery."

President Kabbah responded with an unprecedented proclamation! He

Sierra Leone president Alhaji Dr. Ahmad Tejan Kabbah stands with Thomalind Martin Polite and Priscilla's Homecoming participants following a reception at which he stated he would request Parliament to allow Thomalind and Antawn Polite dual citizenship. Courtesy, Idriss Kpange.

Thomalind and Antawn Polite sit amidst a group of elders during a festive celebration in Dunkegba Village. Courtesy, Alison Sutherland.

Charlie Haffner of the Freetown Players (left), Thomalind Martin Polite, and Manilius Garber (far right) smile ebulliently following a Priscilla's Homecoming reception. Courtesy, Charlie Haffner.

would, he stated, request that Parliament make an exception and begin the process of dual citizenship for the Polites. He also decreed that the picture of Priscilla (created by Charleston artist Dana Coleman) be shown on television daily throughout the remainder of Priscilla's Homecoming and with a short historical narrative about Mrs. Polite "for every Sierra Leonean to see her."

A few days later, Thomalind's comments, as she sat in the Bunce Island female slave yard, were as powerful and uplifting as the words of the old African in "The People Could Fly."

> I did not understand what my father [Thomas Martin] told me [about the importance of family], but now I understand. He was trying to trace the family history before Ed Ball came to us, but he had gotten to a point where he could not go back any further. There were no more records.
>
> And I was in college. I was doing my own thing, and I knew about it. I knew it was important. But not until I became older did I understand what it meant to him then. I [now] feel the same way! I can imagine that's how he felt: very proud!

To African Americans who one day would want to know about her sojourn, Thomalind said she would advise:

> Be proud of who you are because to have come [from so far away] and survived this long, you're strong. Be proud! And explore your own heritage. Try to seek out your family. And if you're not close to your family, get as close as you can. You never know when you'll be separated. (Frazier. Interview with Thomalind Martin Polite at Bunce Island.)

For those who desire to climb higher and higher in making connections with themselves, connections with family members, connections with cultural understanding, Mrs. Polite's words are empowering and worthy of remembering: "Be proud! And explore your own heritage. Try to seek out your family. And if you're not close to your family, get as close as you can. You never know when you'll be separated!"

Artist Dana Coleman of Charleston, South Carolina, created the image of Priscilla by morphing images of Sierra Leonean girls with one of Thomalind at age ten for a family resemblance. He positioned the child captive with her head tilted upward to reflect a spirit of resilience and determination. Courtesy, Dana M. Coleman, www.danacoleman.net.

"I Want to Climb Up Jacob's Ladder"

(Gullah spiritual)

I want to climb up Jacob's ladder, up Jacob's ladder, up Jacob's
    ladder
I want to climb up Jacob's ladder
But I cannot until I make my peace with the Lord
I will praise ye the Lord
I will praise Him til I die
Praise Him by and by in the New Jerusalem

I want to cross the River of Jordan, the River of Jordan, the River
    of Jordan
I want to cross the River of Jordan
But I cannot until I make my peace with the Lord
I will praise ye the Lord
I will praise Him til I die
Praise Him by and by
In the New Jerusalem

I want to climb up higher and higher, up higher and higher, up
    higher and higher
I want to climb up higher and higher
But I cannot until I make my peace with the Lord
I will praise ye the Lord
I will praise Him til I die
Praise Him by and by in the New Jerusalem

I want to climb up Jacob's ladder, up Jacob's ladder, up Jacob's
    ladder
I want to climb up Jacob's ladder
But I cannot until I make my peace with the Lord
I will praise ye the Lord
I will praise Him til I die
Praise Him by and by in the New Jerusalem

Jes keep on prayin. De Lawd is nigh.

In honor of our many cultural commonalities, people should find reasons to celebrate. I participated in many wonderful celebrations during Priscilla's Homecoming. I marveled as the Freetown Players, cultural ambassadors of Sierra Leone, performed original songs throughout our visit. One haunting tune, "Priscilla's Song," was written by the founder of Freetown Players, Charlie Haffner. It proclaims "welcome" to Thomalind in five Sierra Leonean languages: *Kaboh* in Krio; *Unu wali* in Susu; *Sekeh* in Temne; *Bua bisieh* in Mende; *Wali bena* in Limba. *Gbinka Kura Masaba* means "I swear to God," which means "sincerity" in Temne.

The chorus of "Priscilla's Song" resounds:

Kaboh, kaboh Thomalind Martin Polite
Unu wali Thomalind Martin Polite
Sekeh, sekeh bua bisieh
Wali bena o gbinka Kura Masaba

Each verse concludes with the lyrics:

Rush with the message
Go tell it to the people
Open the gates
For Priscilla's coming home!

Priscilla's greatness in bridging cultural impasses was also celebrated onstage at Fourah Bay College during the final night in Sierra Leone. Sierra Leonean playwright and lecturer Raymond DeSouza George used actors to personify the Statue of Liberty and the slave castle on Bunce Island in his play "From Under the Carpet" to explain the horrors of transatlantic slavery.

As recorded by newspaper journalist Herb Frazier of Charleston, South Carolina, who also participated in "Priscilla's Posse,"

> The play spans several generations, beginning with the capture of a girl in Sierra Leone who's sold into slavery in America and later named Priscilla. Polite is Priscilla's seventh-generation granddaughter. It ends with Mama Salone [Mother Sierra Leone], portrayed by Sarah King, being overjoyed when she is reunited with Polite, who was called on the stage to make her feel a part of the play.
>
> With Polite on the stage, Mama Salone said: "She has brought me a new strength. . . . Can your child be dead when you have a grandchild? If Thomalind is here, Priscilla is alive."
>
> But later, Mama Salone falls ill, overcome by all the problems that beset this West African nation, which, according to the United Nations, is the poorest country in the world.
>
> When Polite visits Mama Salone in the hospital, Mama is revived after hearing a confession from the Statue of Liberty, portrayed by George, and Bunce Island, played by Jonathan Bundu.

Charlie Haffner (right) wrote "Priscilla's Song," which welcomed Thomalind Martin Polite in five Sierra Leonean languages. Courtesy, Jacque Metz.

Bunce Island, located deep inside the Freetown harbor, is the site of a 18ᵗʰ-century fortress that shipped enslaved Africans to North America from 1670 to 1808. According to ship records, Priscilla was on a vessel 249 years ago that stopped at Bunce Island before sailing to Charleston.

Bunce Island said, "Mama Salone, I ask you to forgive me. I am your kith and kin, but I was the one who handed over my brothers and sisters into slavery. Please, Mama. Ask Thomalind to forgive me on behalf of Priscilla and all those I betrayed."

But then the Statue of Liberty chimes in. Standing on a raised platform, George said in a booming voice: "You are not the only one guilty of betrayal. Because I have resisted confinement in spite of my fixed roots, I can tell you unequivocally that my eyes have gone globetrotting. I have proof that big brother have nurtured and kept slavery alive."

In an interview, George said, "He who buys and he who sells are equally guilty whatever the motivation. Human beings are not commodities."

He titled the play "From Under the Carpet" because for generations so much about slavery has been hidden." (Frazier, "Play written in honor of woman's visit to Sierra Leone," *The Post and Courier*, Charleston, South Carolina, July 24, 2005, 2F)

The play opened eyes and will bring healing to many.

The most memorable celebration in Sierra Leone—at least, for me—was somewhat serendipitous! Every day there brought emotional, spiritual, and cultural surprises, so I knew to be expectant. Yet I truly wasn't ready for what I witnessed! Our itinerary stated,

DAY SIX (Tuesday, May 31ˢᵗ)
• Depart hotel 8:00 AM
• Day Trip to Kafu Bullom Chiefdom (near Lungi Airport) to see traditional seaside village of Dunkegba, fishing boats, rice farms, yeliba (griot) performance, etc.

This trip proved categorically to be far beyond anything I could have imag-

The celebration at the airport in Freetown, Sierra Leone, began a festive and spirited journey.

An elder pours libation at the airport in Freetown, upon the arrival of Priscilla's Homecoming participants.

Photos by author.

ined. It was a Penn Center Heritage Days festival (St. Helena Island, South Carolina), Georgia Sea Island Festival (St. Simons Island), Gullah Festival (Beaufort, SC), MOJA Festival (Charleston, SC), and Hilton Head Island Gullah Celebration combined *and more!* The day filled me with a spirit of togetherness . . . of wonder . . . of connection with my rice-eating-Geechee heritage . . . of joy like when one has prayed and prayed until one has prayed through.

Driving away from Kafu Bullom Chiefdom and days afterward, I reflected on the experiences of that day trip: dancing with the Elders, watching rice demonstrations, stepping down sand steps to the panoramic vista of a seaside village that I, if I were a resident,

A stilt dancer performs at a festival in Dunkegba Village.

would never want to be torn away from—as Priscilla may have been. The spirit of Africa enveloped me. Each time a memory crystallized, I hummed the tune of a spiritual from my youth—one I had heard at Brick Baptist Church on St. Helena Island: "Jes Keep on Prayin." I had tapped tempo to it with my feet onto wooden floors during Community Sings at Penn Center's Frissell Hall. I had led it on occasions and had felt the wave of *a cappella* voices joining my lead as strongly and as certainly as I'd heard the waves crashing onto the shores at Dunkegba Village. With each wave, I felt a spirit of joy and peace. . . .

"Jes Keep on Prayin."

Jes keep on prayin. De Lawd is nigh.
Jes keep on prayin. He'll hear yo cry.
De Lawd has promist, an His word is true.
Jes keep on prayin. He'll ansa you.

Een de midnight hour, de Lawd is nigh.
Een de midnight hour, He'll hear yo cry.
De Lawd has promist, an His word is true.
Jes keep on prayin. He'll ansa you.

When yo friends forsake you, de Lawd is nigh.
When yo friends forsake you, He'll hear yo cry.
De Lawd has promist, an His word is true.
Jes keep on prayin. He'll ansa you.

When you in trouble, de Lord is nigh.
When you in trouble, He'll hear yo cry.
De Lawd has promist, an His word is true.
Jes keep on prayin. He'll ansa you.

Jes keep on prayin. De Lawd is nigh.
Jes keep on prayin. He'll hear yo cry.
De Lord has promist, an His word is true.
Jes keep on prayin. He'll ansa you.

To that same tune, I composed lyrics to a song about the day's excitement:

In Dunkegba Village, what a time we had!
They threw us a festival that made us proud and glad!

Crowds and crowds of people stood on the roadside.
They shouted, cheered, and grinned when Thomalind rode by.

The Susu Village elders all led the way.
The drummers pounded drums; musicians started to play.

We stepped down a stairway that had been hand-cut in sand.
Drummers stomped; stilt dancers pranced. The merriment was
    grand!

This rice village festival was a sight to see.
It made us glad to know we were from the same family tree!

It's a song of exultation, proclaiming in Gullah that "De African sperit come dong on we—mek we know we dey one an lef we haat in peace!" Translation: "The magic, the beauty, the culture, the hospitality, the splendor of Africa fell upon us like a spiritual awakening—making us know we are one and leaving our hearts in peace."

"In Dunkegba Village, what a time we had!" Courtesy, Leslie Anderson Morales.

"De African Sperit Come Dong on We"
(Sung to the tune of Gullah spiritual "Jes Keep on Prayin")

Een Dunkegba Village, what a time we had!
Dey trow we a festibal. Mek we feel glad glad!
De African Sperit come dong on we.
Mek we know we dey one, an lef we haat een peace.

Courtesy Toni Carrier,
Joyce Reese McCollum,
and Africana Heritage Project,
www.africanaheritage.com.

Courtesy, Jacque Metz.

180

Crowds an crowds ob peepul dem, dey stan pon de roadside.
Dey shout, dey cheer, dey grin when Thomalind ride by.
De African Sperit come dong on we.
Mek we know we dey one, an lef we haat een peace.

Courtesy, Alison Sutherland.

Courtesy, Toni Carrier, Joyce Reese McCollum, and
Africana Heritage Project, www.africanaheritage.com.

De Susu Village eldas dem, dey all lead de way.
De drummas POUND de drums. Musicians staat fa play.
De African Sperit come dong on we.
Mek we know we dey one, an lef we haat een peace.

Courtesy, Idriss Kpange.

Courtesy, Alison Sutherland.

We step dong a stairway handcut een de sand.
Dancas stomp. Stilt dancas prance. De merriment been gran!
De African Sperit come dong on we.
Mek we know we dey one, an lef we haat een peace.

Courtesy, Toni Carrier,
Joyce Reese McCollum,
and Africana Heritage Project,
www.africanaheritage.com.

Dis Rice Village Festibal e beena sight fa see!
E mek we glad fa know we from de same fambly tree!
De African Sperit come dong on we.
Mek we know we dey one, an lef we haat een peace.

De African Sperit come dong on we.
Mek we know we dey one, an lef we haat een peace.

Words by Ronald Daise
© 2005

Photos courtesy, Leslie Anderson Morales.

Reminiscences of MY Sea Island Heritage

The "Saint Helena Hymn" has been a part of my cultural consciousness since childhood. Penned by John Greenleaf Whittier upon the request of Charlotte Forten, Penn School's first black instructor, it was first sung at Brick Baptist Church, St. Helena Island, on Christmas day 1862. I've passed along its message of freedom to many.

In 1983, I met Natalie Eldridge soon after she arrived in Beaufort County from Syracuse, New York, and shared the song's poignancy with her. She had traveled to a community "where people dress loud and talk funny!"—friends and relatives had cautioned her. Her plans were to assist family members for about two weeks, maximum, with her ailing grandmother who had recently relocated to Lady's Island with Natalie's aunt and St. Helena-born uncle-in-law. Hearing the "St. Helena Hymn," evoked a sense of independence within her, and her plans changed.

It was a Friday afternoon, near closing time. We had arrived at the Penn Center campus a few weeks after we met. I was giving her a tour of St. Helena and the surrounding islands. No stranger to Penn Center since childhood, I was deep in research on a book project and regularly pored through photographs at the Penn museum, seeking images to accompany the text. The resulting *Reminiscences of Sea Island Heritage, Legacy of Freedmen on St. Helena Island* was published three years later.

That particular Friday, I asked the secretary for the key to the York W. Bailey Museum (which at that time was housed in the Butler Building) and gave Natalie a personal tour of my community's heritage. Mrs. Agnes C. Sherman, museum coordinator, had a display of "Saint Helena Hymn" lyrics handwritten on several poster boards.

"Want to hear the tune?" I asked Natalie.

"Sure!" she answered.

I proudly sang each verse—*a cappella*, amidst the cultural artifacts. My abil-

This picture is one of the earliest of Ron, at age 4. He's seated on the steps of his family's home in the Cedar Grove community of St. Helena Island, South Carolina. Top row: mother, Kathleen Grant Daise; father, Henry Daise; sister, Vera Daise. Middle: sister, Irene Daise; niece, Marva Carr; Ron; brother, Stanley Daise. Bottom: sister, Barbara Daise. Photo by sister, Mildred Daise, circa 1960.

ity to gain entry to a building at an esteemed cultural institution, along with my rootedness in a community where my parents, grandparents, and great-grandparents have lived, as well as my soloing my community's anthem, endeared me to her, Natalie attests. She says that in coming to Beaufort, she felt she had come home.

In 1985, Natalie became my bride. In 1987, after the publication of my first book, we began singing the "Saint Helena Hymn" and sharing the significance of sea island culture through songs, stories, and dramatizations with audiences around the country. Nick Jr.'s television show *Gullah Gullah Island*, in which we starred and served as cultural consultants, afforded us the unique opportunity to share aspects of heritage as a cultural backdrop to a much wider audience during four years of production (1994–1999) and several years in reruns.

Letters and e-mails from audience members—even comments from passersby on the street—testify that our programs and productions, our art, our journeying have made others revel in the significance of their own personal cultural reminiscences. Sometimes the power of their testaments catches me unawares.

In 2005 as I returned to Freetown aboard a large and very crowded ferry, I marveled at the phenomenon of making cultural connections halfway around the world via a television show that had been broadcast internationally. The trip followed the Priscilla's Homecoming day of celebration and festivities in Dunkegba Village in Kafu Bullom Chiefdom. Many of the "Homecoming" par-

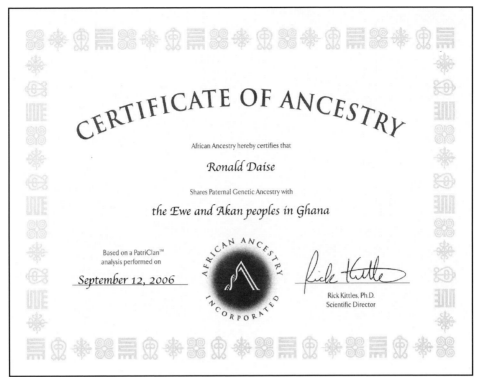

Certificate of paternal lineage based on DNA analysis.

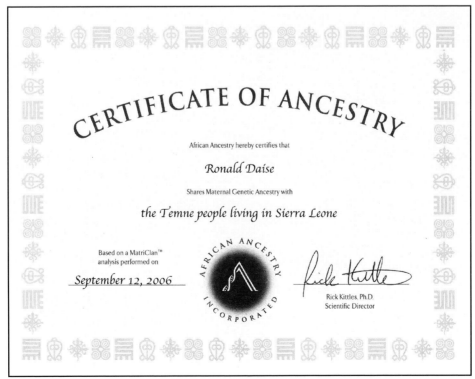

Certificate of maternal lineage based on DNA analysis.

ticipants—dubbed "Priscilla's Posse" by Thomalind and Antawn Polite a few days earlier—were sporting Priscilla's Homecoming T-shirts.

"What's this Priscilla's Homecoming about?" a curious passenger asked.

One of the Posse informed him that the event was a Gullah homecoming.

"Gullah? As in *Gullah Gullah Island*?" the tall stranger responded.

"Yes," Joseph Opala answered. "And the star of that program is right over there!" he continued, pointing in my direction.

The curious passenger turned out to be a Nigerian journalist living and working in Germany. His keen, piercing African eyes and facial features seemed St. Helenian. He had watched the show, he said, with his four-year-old son. Aspects of the production—the family togetherness, the music, the sea island sites, and my speech—reminded him of his homeland. Smiling like long-lost friends, and clasping each other's shoulder as we stood side by side, we posed for a photo to give his son upon his return home.

I was deeply touched with our meeting! Why? Because "there's a connection, deep down in my spirit with Africa. West Africa."

The connections over the years have transcended culture and tapped a quality of life that individuals hold dearly: a sense of individual and collective freedom! As Whittier wrote:

Oh, none in all the world before
Were ever glad as we!
We're free on Carolina's shore,
We're all at home and free.

Thou Friend and Helper of the poor,
Who suffered for our sake,
To open every prison door,
And every yoke to break!

Bend low Thy pitying face and mild,
And help us sing and pray;
The hand that blessed the little child
Upon our foreheads lay.

We hear no more the driver's horn,
No more the whip we fear.
This holy day that saw Thee born
Was never half so dear.

The very oaks are greener clad,
The waters brighter smile;
Oh, never shone a day so glad
On sweet St. Helena's Isle.

We praise Thee in our songs today,
To Thee in prayer we call.
Make swift the feet and straight the way
Of freedom unto all.

Come once again, O blessed Lord!
Come walking on the sea!
And let the mainlands hear the word
That sets the island free!

For Gullah/Geechee people, a newness, an assurance, a liberating essence pervades us when we can say with pride, "Dats Right, I Am a Gullah!"

"Dats Right, I Am a Gullah"

(Sung to the tune of "Children, Go Where I Send Thee," a coded message song used by Harriet Tubman, celebrated conductor of The Underground Railroad)

Dats right, I am a Gullah
A saltwata Geechee-Gullah
This is Reason Number One—
I was born on an island,
a Carolina/Georgia Sea Island
and my ancestas came from West Africa.

Dats right, I am a Gullah
A saltwata Geechee-Gullah
This is Reason Number Two—
I eat hoppin john and other rice dishes, too
One is I was born on an island
a Carolina/Georgia Sea Island
and my ancestas came from West Africa.

Dats right, I am a Gullah
A saltwata Geechee-Gullah
This is Reason Number Three—
Beliefs and oral history
Two is hoppin john and other rice dishes, too
One is I was born on an island,
a Carolina/Georgia Sea Island
and my ancestas came from West Africa

Dats right, I am a Gullah
A saltwata Geechee-Gullah
This is Reason Number Four
Rice and cotton and indigo
Three is beliefs and oral history
Two is hoppin john and other rice dishes, too
One is I was born on an island,
a Carolina/Georgia Sea Island
and my ancestas came from West Africa

Dats right, I am a Gullah
A saltwata Geechee-Gullah
This is Reason Number 10
I look back an rememba my ancestas' strength
Nine is respect for eldas
Eight is de Gullah language
Seven is our spiritual songs about heaven
Six is sweetgrass baskets
Five is benne wafers
Four is cotton, rice, and indigo
Three is beliefs and oral history
Two is hoppin john and other rice dishes, too
One is I was born on an island,
a Carolina/Georgia Sea Island
and my ancestas came from West Africa

I'm Gullah cause my ancestas came from West Africa

Words by Ronald Daise
© 2005

Courtesy, Don Clerico, Charleston Southern University.

Addendum

The following organizations and agencies in Ghana and Sierra Leone, Africa, and in South Carolina, with which I've visited and interacted, welcome charitable donations to maintain their missions and services:

Tuwohofo-Holly International School
ATTN: Mr. Ato Baidoo, Headmaster
Box AD 240
Cape Coast, Ghana (West Africa)

School of African Rhythm and Dance
ATTN: Letitia Araba Mensah
P.O. Box 120
Cape Coast, Ghana
TELEPHONE: 233-042-33527
E-MAIL: letitiaaraba@yahoo.com

The Ballanta Academy of Music
27 Liverpool St.
Freetown, Sierra Leone
TELEPHONE: 232-22-227743
E-MAIL: ballanta1996@yahoo.co.uk

Bunce Island Preservation Initiative
c/o National Tourist Board
P.O. Box 1435
Cape Sierra Hotel
Aberdeen
Freetown, Sierra Leone
TELEPHONE: 232-22-236620
FAX: 232-22-236621
E-MAIL: bipisalone@yahoo.com

Freetown Players International
56 Dundas Street
Freetown, Sierra Leone
TELEPHONE: 232-76-721252
www.freetongplayers.com

Brookgreen Gardens
ATTN: Development Office
P.O. Box 2092
Pawleys Island, SC 29585
TELEPHONE: 843-235-6000
www.brookgreen.org

DreamKeepers Community Art Center
ATTN: Mr. David Drayton
P.O. Box 1507
Georgetown, SC 29442
TELEPHONE: 343-546-1974

Penn Center, Inc.
ATTN: History and Culture Program
P.O. Box 126
St. Helena Island, SC 29920
TELEPHONE: 843-838-2432
www.penncenter.com

The Belle W. Baruch Foundation
Hobcaw Barony
22 Hobcaw Road
Georgetown, SC 29440
TELEPHONE: 843-546-4623
www.hobcawbarony.org

Fort Sumter National Monument
1214 Middle Street
Sullivan's Island, SC 29482
843-883-3123
www.nps.gov/fosu

The International African American Museum
ATTN: Dr. Gretta Middleton, Director
P.O. Box 20069
Charleston, SC 29413
TELEPHONE: 843-724-3776
www.charlestoncity.info/iaam
E-MAIL: iaam@ci.charleston.sc.us

The West Africa Council of South Carolina
c/o The Corporation for Economic Opportunity (CEO)
ATTN: Joseph J. James, President & CEO
116 Wildewood Club Court
Columbia, SC 29223
TELEPHONE: 803-462-0153
www.prosperityforall.org

Photo by author.

Courtesy, Don Clerico, Charleston Southern University.

Sources Cited

"Bunce Island Preservation Initiative" brochure. National Tourist Board of Sierra Leone. 2005.

Dabbs, Edith M. *Face of an Island.* Columbia, SC: The R.L. Bryan, Co. 1970.

Daise, Ron and Natalie. *Feel Like Journey On: Songs and Stories of Gullah Heritage (audio recording).* G.O.G. Enterprises, 1993. www.gullahgullah.com

Daise, Ronald. "Brookgreen Gardens Lowcountry Trail: A Connecting of History." *Brookgreen Journal* (Volume XXXV/Number 2, November 2005): 8-9.

————. "Lowcountry Trail Dedication." *Brookgreen Journal* (Volume XXXVI/Number 1, June 2006): 8-9.

————. "Layered Meanings; Multiple Truths." Electronic document www.csuniv.edu/ghana/index.asp

————. *Little Muddy Waters: A Gullah Folk Tale.* Beaufort, SC: G.O.G. Enterprises, 1997.

————. "Pageantry: Ghanaian Festivals & Celebrations." Electronic document www.csuniv.edu/ghana/index.asp.

————. *Reminiscences of Sea Island Heritage: Legacy of Freedmen on St. Helena Island.* Orangeburg, SC: Sandlapper Publishing, inc., 1986.

De Good Nyews Wa John Write: The Gospel according to John in Gullah (Sea Island *Creole*). Waxhaw, NC: Wycliffe Bible Translators, 2003.

De Nyew Testament: The New Testament in Gullah. New York: American Bible Society, 2005.

Derrick, Hope. "Congressman Clyburn Introduces Gullah/Geechee Cultural Heritage Act" News Release, July 12, 2004. Electronic document www.house.gov/apps/list/press/sc06_clyburn/041712Gullahbill.html

Frazier, Herb. "Audio Interview with Antawn Polite at Bunce Island, Sierra Leone, on May 28, 2005."

————. "Audio Interview with Thomalind Martin Polite at Bunce Island, Sierra Leone, on May 28, 2005."

————. "Play written in honor of woman's visit to Sierra Leone." Charleston, SC: *The Post and Courier* (July 24, 2005): 2F.

"Gullah culture study complete." Beaufort, SC: *The Beaufort Gazette* (December 27, 2005): 3A.

Haffner, Charlie. Personal communication, "Hello from Freetown—the mosquitoes are safe and well." Electronic Document chafaf99@yahoo.com to rdaise@brookgreen.org, July 22, 2005.

Hamilton, Virgina. *The People Could Fly: American Black Folktales.* New York: Alfred A. Knopf, 1985.

The Language You Cry In: The Story of a Mende Song. Producer/Directors Alvaro Toepke and Angel Serrano, Narrator Vertamae Grosvenor, California Newsreel Distri., 1998.

Lightbody, Arthur. "JAARS Hosts Celebration for the Completion of The Gullah New Testament" News Release, October 17, 2005. Electronic document www.jaars.org, arthur_lightbody@sil.org

"Low Country Gullah Culture Special Resource Study (Public Review Draft)." National Park Service, U.S. Department of the Interior, December 2003.

Nichols, Elaine ed. *"The Last Miles of the Way: African-American Homegoing Traditions 1980-Present.* Columbia, SC: South Carolina State Museum, 1989.

Opala, Joseph. "More and More Specific…" Electronic document www.yale.edu/glc/priscilla/opala.htm.

———. *The Gullah: Rice, Slavery, and the Sierra Leone-American Connection.* Freetown, Sierra Leone: United States Information Service, 1988.

"Omnibus Ars Musica" brochure, The Ballanta Academy of Music. 2005.

Tibbetts, John H. "Gullah's Radiant Light," *Coastal Heritage* 1993 (Winter 2004-05). SC Sea Grant Consortium, Charleston, SC.

Websites about Ghana:
www.ghanatourism.gov.gh/main/index.asp
www.worldandi.com/specialreport/panafest/panafest.html
www.internationalspecialreports.com/africa/01/ghana/tourism/index.html
www.sunseekerstours.com/files/home.html

Websites about Priscilla's Homecoming:
www.yale.edu/glc/priscilla/
www.africanaheritage.com/Priscillas_Homecoming.asp
www.charlestonmag.com/pop_archive1.html
www.danacoleman.net/aboutpriscilla.php

Wood, Betty C. *Slavery in Colonial Georgia.* Athens, GA: University of Georgia Press, 1984.

——— and Thomas Stephens. "The Introduction of Black Slavery in Georgia. *Georgia Historical Quarterly 58* (Spring 1974): 24-40."

Wright, Logie E. ed. "Shine Like De Mornin' Star: N.G.J. Ballanta of Sierra Leone, Composer and Ethnomusicologist." United States Information Agency, 1995.

Photos courtesy, Don Clerico, Charleston Southern University.

Photos courtesy, Don Clerico,
Charleston Southern University.